'THE SERVANT OF THE LORD'

THE
'SERVANT OF THE LORD'

BY

ROBERT H. KENNETT, D.D.

CANON OF ELY AND REGIUS PROFESSOR OF HEBREW IN THE
UNIVERSITY OF CAMBRIDGE; FELLOW OF QUEENS' COLLEGE
AUTHOR OF 'IN OUR TONGUES,' ETC

WIPF & STOCK · Eugene, Oregon

Wipf and Stock Publishers
199 W 8th Ave, Suite 3
Eugene, OR 97401

The Servant of the Lord
By Kennett, Robert H.
ISBN 13: 978-1-60608-391-8
Publication date 12/30/2008
Previously published by Edward Arnold, 1911

TO MY CHILDREN

הנה נחלת יהוה בנים שכר פרי הבטן:

PREFACE

THE four lectures contained in this volume were originally delivered as one course of the lectures arranged for the Clergy in Cambridge in the Long Vacation of 1909. The subject itself needs no apology, for few will deny that those passages of the book of Isaiah which treat of 'The Servant of the Lord' are among the most important of the Old Testament Scriptures. Not only is our whole conception of prophecy generally affected by the interpretation of these passages which we may adopt; our view of the Atonement largely depends upon the sense which we assign to the words: 'He was wounded for our transgressions.' It is therefore of extreme importance that we should endeavour to discover the meaning which these passages would naturally bear in the age in which they were composed; in other words, that we should study them in the light of the history of the Church of Israel. This, however, is a by no means easy task. It requires no small mental effort to analyse minutely words and phrases which have long been part of our devotional equipment, and many will shrink from subjecting that which is associated in their minds with the holiest mysteries to anything of the nature of a critical scrutiny. But inasmuch as our traditional way of regarding prophecy often completely ignores phrases which must originally have had *some* meaning, and inasmuch as prophecy and that which is regarded as its fulfilment are not unfrequently harmonised only by wresting the plain grammatical sense of Scripture, it is surely in the highest degree desirable that we should seek to discover what the plain grammatical sense may be. No exposition of prophecy can be satisfactory which does not do justice to *every translatable clause*. This canon of interpretation, however, can only be applied by determining what is translatable, and in this respect the textual criticism of the Old Testament still leaves much to be desired. It is remarkable that whereas nowadays no one of ordinary intelligence would dream of upholding the so-called *textus receptus* of the New Testament, it is not yet generally recognised that the *textus receptus* of the Old Testament has no greater claim to our respect. Many people are, indeed, prepared to recognise the existence of corruption in the Hebrew text where the LXX. witnesses to an undoubtedly superior reading, but there are not a few who are loth to admit any error on any other evidence—thus virtually maintaining that the Hebrew text was perfect at the time when the LXX. version was made. This, however, cannot be admitted by any one who has been brought up to reverence grammar. If the clearest, most strongly marked rules of grammar can be set at nought —as we must believe, if the Masoretic text be correct—then exact study of the Old Testament becomes impossible, and it is idle to appeal to the teaching of Scripture.

There may, however, be some who, though they fully recognise the textual difficulties of the Old Testament, are somewhat shocked by what they consider the unnecessary analysis of whole chapters of prophecy into mere collections of fragments. This, no doubt, will be especially the case with those who are unable to study the original Hebrew, and depend only upon the English versions. But since there is a tendency in a translation to soften down abrupt transitions of thought, and to remove grammatical difficulties, it is obvious that a version is inadequate to supply *criteria* of analysis. I would therefore ask my readers to remember that my own anaylsis is based everywhere on the original Hebrew. At the same time I would insist upon the parallel between the books of the Prophets and the Synoptic Gospels. If it be conceded that whole sections of the Gospels are composed of fragments, what *à priori* improbability is there in the proposition that many sections of the Prophets are similarly composed? The problems which present themselves in the study of the Gospels are indeed very similar to those which occur in the study of the Prophets. It has been disastrous to the understanding of the Bible that investigation into the historical meaning of the Old and New Testaments has so frequently been carried on 'in watertight compartments.' If we understand the manner of life and teaching of 'Jesus of Nazareth which was a Prophet,' we shall be in a better position to understand the manner of life and teaching of the Prophets who prepared His way before Him. There is no chasm between the two Testaments. 'The New is the continuation of the Old.

ROBERT H. KENNETT.

QUEENS' COLLEGE, CAMBRIDGE,
   Feast of the Conversion of S. Paul, 1911.

CONTENTS

		PAGE
LECTURE I	. . . . .	1
,, II	. . . . .	29
,, III	. . . . .	61
,, IV	. . . . .	95

THE SERVANT OF THE LORD

LECTURE I

THOSE passages of the book of Isaiah which speak of the 'Servant of the Lord,' of which the greatest and most familiar is Isaiah lii. 13-liii., are generally regarded as the climax of Old Testament prophecy. The passage just mentioned has so many points of contact with what Christians believe concerning the Christ who suffered for our sins and rose again for our justification, that it could not fail to arrest the attention of Christians. 'It looks,' as Delitzsch has said, 'as if it had been written beneath the cross upon Golgotha, and was illuminated by the heavenly brightness of the full שֵׁב לִימִינִי.'[1] That in this passage we have language which may be applied to Christ, and indeed is 'fulfilled,' that is to say, finds its fullest meaning, in Him, no one who is a Christian will deny.

[1] *i.e.* 'Sit thou on my right hand' (Ps. cx. 1).

On the other hand, both the express teaching of the Old Testament itself [1] and commonsense require us to believe that it had an intelligible meaning when it was first composed. The problem, therefore, which lies before us is to discover some period in the history of Israel when these words would have borne a plain meaning, at least to all spiritually-minded men. If we can determine what they meant to those to whom they were first uttered, we shall have a clearer conception of the scope of their meaning as applied to Christ.

Unfortunately this is by no means an easy matter. Careful literary criticism of the book of Isaiah reveals the extraordinary complexity of its composition. Throughout the book, but especially in the last twenty-seven chapters, passages of entirely different *provenance* and date are placed in juxtaposition. A careful scrutiny will frequently make it plain that even in sections which deal with the same subject we have the work of more than one author, or at least a combination

---

[1] Thus Deuteronomy xviii. 21 f. makes it clear that a prophet was expected to speak of things, the verification of which was within the power of his hearers.

THE SERVANT OF THE LORD 3

of passages which did not originally belong to the same context. Thus, for example, in Isaiah xlii. 1-7 we have a prophecy relating to the 'Servant of the Lord' which a casual reader might imagine to be homogeneous. A closer examination, however, will show that vv. 5-7 did not originally follow upon vv. 1-4; for in vv. 1-4 Jehovah Himself is the speaker, and speaks of the 'Servant' in the third person; in vv. 5-7 Jehovah is spoken of in the third person as directly addressing the 'Servant.' This is but one instance of a phenomenon which is apparent throughout the latter portion of the book. It would appear that the final editor was concerned rather to arrange the fragmentary prophecies which lay before him in some sort of order which would make them serve as Church lessons than to discover their original connection.

But this being the case, it is evident that the mere position of a section in the book affords no indication of its date. The student of Isaiah finds himself somewhat in the position of an antiquary who is endeavouring to date the materials of an Elizabethan house which has been constructed out of the stones of some dismantled abbey. In the wall of such a house there may occur in juxtaposition stones which originally occupied widely different positions in the building that was used as a quarry. Often there will be no clue as to the original site of such stones, but in many cases the character of the hewing or carving will reveal the date; and sometimes it will be possible to determine the original use. This illustration is, perhaps, sufficient to show the injustice of calling such a process of literary analysis 'destructive criticism.' One does not *destroy* a house, or render it unfit for the purpose for which it is intended, by the attempt to assign dates to the materials of which it is composed.

We may then examine the composition of those passages of the book of Isaiah which speak of the 'Servant of the Lord,' without bias as to any particular author or date, except, of course, that we cannot place them later than the time at which we are compelled by the Septuagint translation to believe the whole book to have been in existence.

It is generally recognised that these passages are four[1] in number; xlii. 1-7, xlix. 1-12,

[1] There is, it is true, one other passage which bears some

THE SERVANT OF THE LORD 5

l. 4-9, lii. 13-liii. As I have already stated they are not homogeneous, though they all

resemblance to the 'Servant' passages, chap. lxi. 1 ff., and which, according to the literal sense of the words, has the best claim to be called 'Messianic,' inasmuch as the speaker claims that the Lord has anointed him. In this passage, however, the speaker appears merely as the herald of a salvation which will restore happiness to the miserable and liberty to the prisoners. There is no evidence that he himself has shared in the sufferings of those whom he comforts. Since in xlv. 1 Cyrus is called the Lord's 'anointed,' it is not improbable that this section in its original connection was a soliloquy put into his mouth (cf. the language which is ascribed to Cyrus in Ezra i. 2 ff.). Inasmuch as Ben Sira, who probably quotes this passage (Ecclus. xlviii. 24), apparently understood it to be spoken by Isaiah himself, it is evident that in the recension of the book with which he was acquainted, as in the present text, there was nothing to indicate the speaker. But though Ben Sira might have quoted Micah iii. 8 and other passages in support of his view, it must be admitted that the reference to the anointing of the speaker, whoever he may be, is against this interpretation. The anointing of a prophet, it is true, is mentioned in 1 Kings xix. 16, and is apparently implied in Ps. cv. 15; but we have no reason to suppose that prophets were anointed as a rule, unless, perhaps, as in the case of Elisha who was thus constituted the successor of Elijah, to fill some definite position. It is difficult to believe that a post-exilic *anointed* prophet would be anonymous. On the whole, therefore, it seems to be the most probable supposition that words which were originally put into the mouth of Cyrus, having been severed from their original context, were preserved as containing a message of consolation for Israel, and were regarded as the prophet's own account of his mission. In the last revision of the book of Isaiah it is probable that this section, since it is placed after the 'Servant' passages, was regarded as an utterance of the Servant himself.

exhibit a striking similarity in thought, and evidently present the same view of the mission which is fulfilled by the 'Servant.'

Now the first question which naturally presents itself is this : Was the 'Servant of the Lord' a more or less definite conception existing in Israel through several ages, comparable to that of the 'Messiah' or 'The Prophet,' which we find existing in New Testament times, or was it a term applied in this connection only by the writer or writers of the passages which I have enumerated ? In other words ; Ought we to consider the term 'Servant of the Lord' as virtually a proper name, or merely a name descriptive of any one who happens to stand in some special relation to Jehovah ? This question is best answered by reference to the usage of the Old Testament. Etymologically considered, the word 'servant' (עֶבֶד) merely denotes one who performs some sort of work, and, though it may be used of a bondservant, it does not imply the condition of degradation which we associate with the word 'slave.'[1]

---

[1] It may be remembered that English-speaking slave-owners used to speak of their slaves as 'servants,' and did not use the word *slave*.

THE SERVANT OF THE LORD

In an age when parents could sell their children, and a man might be seized for debt, and sold, it is obvious that there was no stigma attached to slavery. It was no more disgraceful among the Hebrews to be a 'servant,' even though a *bondservant*, than it is among us to be a domestic servant. As far as his physical comforts went, it is probable that the condition of the bondservant was superior to that of the *hireling*, who had to work even harder than the slave to keep body and soul together, and whose employer had no special interest in keeping him in good health. But inasmuch as service of this kind, even under favourable conditions, necessarily deprived a man of freedom of action, it was but natural that the term 'servant' -(עֶבֶד) should be used when it was necessary to denote the ideas which we associate with slavery. Thus Egypt during the forced sojourn of the Israelites is described as a 'place [literally "house"] of servants'; but the bad sense which the term 'servants' has here is due to the fact that the *master* is a *foreign* king. An Israelite would have felt no objection to describe himself as a servant of his own king; and, indeed, a king's courtiers and highest ministers of state are always so described. If then we apply to the term 'servant' in the phrase 'Servant of the Lord' the meaning which it has elsewhere, it will mean either one who, whether willingly or otherwise, acknowledges Jehovah as his supreme ruler, or one who is employed by Jehovah to accomplish some work which He will have done. Thus a title which was naturally applied to such men as Abraham, Moses, Joshua, Caleb, David, Eliakim, Isaiah, Zerubbabel, or the looked-for 'Shoot' from the cut-down stump of the dynasty of David, could also be used of one who, like Nebuchadnezzar, was employed by Jehovah to accomplish the chastisement of the stiff-necked nations of Palestine which He had willed. We must be on our guard against the too common assumption that phrases in the Bible have always exactly the same *nuance*. Moreover a designation which may be perfectly suitable in some particular contingency may be positively untrue if regarded as possessing an absolutely general force. Thus a prophet who hoped that Cyrus would lead the flock of Jehovah to their old pasturage, the land of Palestine,

THE SERVANT OF THE LORD 9

with reference to this hope described him, not unnaturally, as 'the shepherd' of Jehovah. Similarly in an age which believed that Hazael had once been anointed by a prophet of Jehovah to chastise His rebellious people, it was a natural metaphor by which Cyrus, who like Hazael was carrying out Jehovah's purpose, though a purpose of love, not chastisement, was described as the 'anointed of Jehovah.'

That the term 'servant of Jehovah' should be applied most frequently to men like Moses, the traditional founder of the Law upon which Jehovah had set the stamp of His approval, or David, the founder of a dynasty which by its permanence appeared to be specially favoured of Jehovah, is only what we should expect. The very fact that the term was constantly applied to both these men, certainly from the Exile onwards, shows that there could not have been at the same time in Israel any common expectation of a deliverer yet to come who bore as his only designation the name 'Servant of the Lord.' It is probable that in every case the meaning of the term was made apparent by the context. We must therefore regard the term 'servant of the Lord,' in the prophecies before us, as a mere *epithet* applied to one, whether an individual or the personification of a nation or section of a nation, who stands in the same sort of relation to Jehovah as Moses or David, Isaiah or Zerubbabel; and we must discover from the context who it is to whom this designation is applied in these passages.

Happily this is an easy matter, for in chap. xlix. 3 the speaker declares that Jehovah has said to him, 'Thou art my servant; Israel, in whom I will be glorified'; and even though we should accept the unnecessary supposition that Israel is a gloss in this place, the close parallelism between the passage before us and chap. xliv. 21-23, in which Israel is declared to be the Lord's servant in whom he will glorify Himself, would prove the correctness of the gloss. But though the section xlix. 1-6 may be regarded as proving the identity of the 'Servant' with Israel, it proves also that the Israel here contemplated is not simply the Israelite nation; for the 'Servant' declares that he has been created by Jehovah, not only to be a light to the Gentiles, but also *to restore Israel*. It is

THE SERVANT OF THE LORD

evident, therefore, that the speaker, though he has a claim to be considered Israel, is not the *whole* of Israel after the flesh, but one who corresponds, as Israel after the flesh does not correspond, to the idea which Jehovah has had in mind in the call and election of Israel. It is plain that the writer of this passage believed that the choice of Israel was no arbitrary act of favouritism on the part of Jehovah, but that Israel had been chosen, as the prophets had been chosen, to fulfil in some special way Jehovah's will. We shall accordingly be in a better position to understand what is here meant, if we trace out the development in Israel of the consciousness of a national mission in the world.

We may take as the starting point of our inquiry the earliest prophet of whose teaching we have definite knowledge. Amos regards Israel as standing in a unique position with reference to Jehovah. Jehovah, he maintains, has 'known' Israel alone of all the families of the earth. The reason why Jehovah has 'known' Israel in this special way is not clearly stated; but the prophet seems to imply that Jehovah has brought Israel into this unique position of privilege with a view to making it a righteous nation, a servant profitable in the eyes of his master, whom indeed his master may treat rather as a son than as a servant. Amos declares that, on the one hand, Jehovah has a special claim on Israel's gratitude, inasmuch as He has brought the people out of the land of Egypt, has led them through the wilderness, has destroyed the Amorites before them, has given them the land of Canaan, and has also raised up of their sons for prophets and of their young men for Nazarites, and that, on the other hand, He has sought by successive chastisements, famine, pestilence, and defeat, to bring them to a better mind. The condition of Israel at the time of Amos made it scarcely possible for the prophet to dwell on Jehovah's purpose for Israel, but the passages to which I have referred make it evident that he himself did ascribe a purpose to Jehovah. It might perhaps be argued from Amos iii. 9 ff., that the prophet considered it the special function of Israel to set an example to the nations, but the passage is too rhetorical to base an argument upon it.

Our next witness is the prophet Hosea, whose idea of Jehovah's choice of Israel,

THE SERVANT OF THE LORD 13

though differently expressed, appears to be essentially the same as that which, we have seen, was held by Amos. For Hosea teaches that Jehovah has chosen Israel as a man chooses his wife, and that He desires to be faithfully loved by Israel as a man desires to be faithfully loved by his wife. He implies that it is Jehovah's will that Israel should be in Jehovah's land all that a good wife is in the home of her husband.

A little later we find Isaiah (i. 24-27) looking for the purification of his people. The genuine Isaianic passages of the book, it must be remembered, probably represent a very small amount of the teaching actually delivered by the prophet; and there is no evidence in them of any consciousness that Jehovah has had a special purpose in the choice of Israel. That such a thought would not, however, be foreign to Isaiah's way of thinking may be fairly argued from his teaching on the subject of the Assyrian. Since Isaiah regarded the Assyrian as an instrument in Jehovah's hand to chastise His rebellious people, and therefore considered that Jehovah manifested His purpose even in the history of the heathen, it is but reasonable to suppose

14   THE SERVANT OF THE LORD

that He assigned to Jehovah also a purpose for Israel.

The teaching of Jeremiah in this respect, while it resembles to a great extent that of his predecessors, may perhaps be regarded as marking a certain advance. For Jeremiah seems to have perceived the solidarity of Israel and the surrounding nations in a somewhat greater degree than previous prophets. The language of the prophecy founded on the visit to the potter (chap. xviii. 7-10) perhaps implies that the prophet hoped that his teaching might bear fruit beyond the border of Israel proper. The same inference may perhaps be drawn from the description of the prophet's call (chap. i. 10). If this inference be correct, and a Hebrew prophet really hoped that his teaching might influence other nations, it is evident that we have the germ of a belief in a mission for Israel, though for a long time to come it was destined to remain only a germ.

Jeremiah's younger contemporary, Ezekiel, though he seems to recognise that the other nations may have true prophets among them (chap. xxxiii. 2-6), and though he has the highest sense of the responsibility resting

THE SERVANT OF THE LORD 15

upon all prophets (*ib.* 6 ff.), gives no indication of any hope that the teaching which emanates from Israel may influence the nations. He looks forward indeed to the time when the nations of the world will recognise the greatness of Jehovah by reason of His work for Israel (xxxvi. 35, 36; xxxvii. 28), but he looks rather for Jehovah's vengeance on the nations than for their conversion.

In the book of Deuteronomy, which is probably to be dated some time during the generation which ended with the appointment of Zerubbabel, we find, as in Ezekiel, the expectation of the destruction of the heathen (cf. vii. 24), who are here regarded as thoroughly bad (cf. ix. 5; xviii. 9 ff.), but there are also some slight indications of a consciousness that Israel may influence the world (cf. iv. 6; xxix. 24 ff.).

A few years later we find the prophet Haggai expecting that the treasures (the desirable things) of all nations will be brought to Jerusalem (ii. 7), but this is to be the result of a shaking of the nations, *i.e.* of a political convulsion of the world, not of the conversion of the nations.

16 THE SERVANT OF THE LORD

Zechariah also expects that a time will come when many nations will join themselves to the Lord (ii. 11 ; viii. 21, 23), if the verses in question be genuine ; he looks, however, not for the conversion of Babylon but for the Lord's vengeance upon it (cf. v. 11 ; vi. 8).

The prophet Malachi, whose date, though it cannot be determined with certainty, is probably about the middle of the fifth century B.C., shows an extraordinary liberality of thought with reference to the Gentiles (cf. i. 11, 14) ; he does not, however, give any indication of a belief that Israel is charged with any mission to the Gentiles.

The memoirs of Nehemiah and the Priestly Code, which was published probably in 433 B.C., are concerned solely with the relation of Israel to Jehovah. Here we find no indication of any thought that Israel possesses any obligations towards the heathen. This is, indeed, only what we should expect from the exigencies of the time ; for Nehemiah could scarcely have dwelt upon Israel's mission to the Gentiles at the time when he was doing his utmost to keep his people from all contact with the Gentiles.

To sum up, therefore, we may say that

THE SERVANT OF THE LORD 17

though in the Scriptures composed up to, and including, the time of Nehemiah there are occasionally seen flashes of a dim consciousness that the other nations of the world as well as Israel are the object of Jehovah's care, these flashes never develop into a steady light. During the whole period covered by the Law, Israel's greatest teachers appear to have taught that Jehovah had separated Israel from the other nations of the earth, not by way of training Israel to be a missionary to those nations, but in order that there might be one nation which Jehovah might claim for His inheritance, His own possession, and on which He might look with pleasure ; or, to adopt a metaphor from Isaiah, that Israel might be to Him a vineyard, carefully cultivated and free from weeds, in which He might find the fruit which He desired.

But if the circumstances of Nehemiah's age made it impossible for him to give his people a sense of responsibility towards the Gentiles, he did succeed in teaching what was equally important to them and ultimately to the world, viz. the conception of a *Church*. In the days of the Kings religion had been an affair of the nation. Those who did not conform to such religion as the king willed could be punished by him as rebels whose very existence endangered the stability of the state. Nehemiah came, not indeed with a new religion, but with a new Law, and a far more stringent interpretation of law. He himself realised the magnitude of the demands which he was making of his people, and he evidently perceived that it would be practically impossible to induce all those who in his days professed and called themselves Jews to take upon them the burden of this law. He determined, therefore, to form what in these days we should call a *league* of those who would pledge themselves to be loyal to the law which he was publishing. A formal document was drawn up to which the leaders both of the priesthood and of the laity affixed their seals. In this way there arose a conception of a congregation, a *Church*, which was not coextensive with the nation. No doubt this conception lost some of its force from the fact that, inasmuch as Nehemiah seems to have made intolerable the position of those people whom he regarded as undesirable, the nation was, at least to a considerable degree, limited to those who had

THE SERVANT OF THE LORD 19

become members of the Church. But an idea that has once taken hold of people's minds is not easily forgotten though for a time it may cease to be prominent. Moreover, the Samaritan schism must have been a reminder to the Jews that not all those who had claimed to be Israel could rightly be regarded as members of the Church, which alone corresponded to the true idea of Israel. The separation of the sheep from the goats, which Nehemiah had carried into practice, would remain the ideal of those who classed themselves among the sheep; and thus would arise the conception of a Church within a Church, the development of which in after time was to prove the climax of Old Testament prophecy.

Exactly a century elapsed between the publication of the Law by Nehemiah and the conquest of Palestine by Alexander the Great in 332. Of this century the history is almost an absolute blank. We know, indeed, that some time between 433 and 408 the Samaritans, who had originally recognised Jerusalem as the one legitimate sanctuary, separated from the Jews and built a rival temple on Mount Gerizim, of which Manasseh, the grandson of the Jewish High Priest Eliashib, became High Priest. The schism, however, appears to have been confined to the province of Samaria proper. The Jews dwelling among the heathen in Galilee and Gilead, who appear to have accepted the Deuteronomic law in the sixth century, seem to have continued loyal to Jerusalem. The only other incidents during this century (*i.e.* 433-332) which are known to us are, (1) the appeals made by the Jews of Elephantine for help to rebuild their temple, first (in 411) to the High Priest John, and then (in 408) to Bagoas, the Persian Governor of Judah, and to Delaiah and Shelamiah, the sons of Sanballat, Governor of Samaria; (2) the High Priest John's murder of his brother Jesus in the Temple, which Bagoas made a pretext for levying a heavy tribute on the daily sacrifices; (3) the transportation of a detachment of Jews to Hyrcania and Babylonia during Artaxerxes Ochus's campaign against Egypt about 351 B.C. On the strength of these last two incidents (of which, however, the former belongs to the time of Artaxerxes Mnemon, not Artaxerxes Ochus) a gigantic theory has been built up of a religious

THE SERVANT OF THE LORD

persecution of the Jews by Artaxerxes Ochus. But though there were extensive risings in Palestine against Ochus, there is nothing to show that the Jews were involved in these, nor are we justified in arguing that any rising in which the Jews took part must of necessity have had a religious character. There is nothing specially to connect the Jews who were transported to the east with Judah, and the bitter animosity which existed at this period between the Jews and the Samaritans makes it unlikely that the Jews made common cause with their deadly enemies even against the hated power of Persia.

It is certainly more probable that the period from 433 to 332 was comparatively uneventful than that it was a time of storm and stress which proved to be the birth throes of a new, and sound, theology. Not that it was without importance for the religion of Israel; far from it. The law which Nehemiah had published could not have its perfect work until it had been assimilated, and the process of assimilation was necessarily one involving time. Perhaps I may be allowed to give a very homely illustration of what I believe the apparently barren period from Nehemiah to Alexander to have done for the Jews. When a freshman comes up to the University from school, and devotes himself to a new study, he lives during his first three terms in a new mental atmosphere. New ideas are presented to him, and it may well be that he scarcely perceives the relation of these to one another, or to the ideas which he has held in the past. But during the Long Vacation he will, if he is a serious student, revise and consolidate the work of the previous year; he will perceive the real significance of teaching which he has hitherto accepted merely as bare fact. If his mental growth at the University is to be divided into a number of definite stages, the first milestone, so to speak, will be not at the end of the third term, but at the end of the Long Vacation. In like manner, if I may apply my illustration, the period between Nehemiah and Alexander was, as it were, the Long Vacation following the time of Nehemiah's novel teaching. Outwardly it might seem barren, but the end of it was a real landmark in the history of Israel. I suppose that we are all conscious of a certain unsuitability in the use of the term *Jew* to denote the inhabitants of Judah in the days,

THE SERVANT OF THE LORD 23

say, of Jeremiah. By a *Jew* we understand not merely one who is a descendant of those who were inhabitants of Judah in the days of the Hebrew Kings, but one who is marked out as distinct from other members of the Semitic race by certain characteristics of religion. If then we are asked to assign a date to the change by which the Hebrews developed into what we should call *Jews*, we may, I think, fairly well point to the hundred years ending 332 B.C. The people of Judah and Jerusalem, when Alexander conquered Palestine, may be fairly accurately described as Jews.

It is probable that the rise of synagogues may be traced to the period following the publication of the law in 433. For so complex a document as the Pentateuch could not be made the rule of life by uneducated people, however devout they might be, unless they received systematic instruction in it. It is probable that it was in order to give this systematic instruction that the synagogues were founded, which were destined to have so powerful an influence on the subsequent development of Judaism.

With the coming of Alexander the Great a new era opened for the Jews. Hitherto they had felt themselves in bondage under the rigorous rule of Persia. Under foreign governors such as Bagoas, and under priests such as John, whose lips did not keep knowledge, it was but natural that those who were zealous for the Law which Nehemiah had set before them should feel themselves to be living in isolation from a world which lay altogether in wickedness, and that they should look with passionate longing for the time which Malachi had predicted, when they that feared the Lord should trample down the wicked under the soles of their feet, as heavy stall-fed oxen, the heaviest animals with which Malachi was acquainted, trample flat that upon which they tread. It would have been strange if, considering their circumstances, the Jews had not looked for vengeance on the heathen rather than for their conversion.

But with the coming of Alexander a happier state of things was brought about. The Jews were now no longer at a disadvantage compared with their heathen neighbours. If they had not obtained national independence, they had at any rate obtained a large measure of political freedom. Moreover, the old barriers had been broken. The world was opened up as it had never been before, and there was no external hindrance to the Jew who wished to take his part in the great development of commerce which Alexander's unification of the world had made possible.

But many of those who for a century had been 'shut up under the law' would be likely to look askance at commercial enterprise which would bring Jews into closer contact with the detested Gentiles. To such people it would doubtless seem that the Holy Land was the only spot in which a Jew might lawfully make his home, and that if, for the present, life there was hard, in due course Jehovah would shake the nations so that their wealth should become the property of Israel. It is this temper which we see illustrated in the character of Jonah, as he is described in the great allegory of that name. Jonah, who is a type of the Jewish nation, recognises no obligations towards the Gentiles; he would rather avoid all contact with them. He shrinks from the suggestion that the Gentiles may listen to the preaching of repentance. He has no desire to see them repentant, for he feels that their past sins have been so enormous that they have no claim to share with the Jews in Jehovah's love. The conversion of the heathen will, he feels, put the Gentiles on an equality with the Jews, an equality for which he has no desire. He looks for the vindication of Israel not through the performance by Israel of the mission for which the nation has been called, but through the destruction of the Gentiles.

If, as is probable, the book of Jonah belongs to the time of Alexander the Great, and is a rebuke of the exclusive spirit of Judaism, and an appeal to the Jews to recognise the Gentiles as objects with them of Jehovah's care and love, we are able to date sufficiently accurately the beginning of a consciousness of a mission in the chosen people. We cannot of course date an intellectual movement as we can date some definite historical event. Even if we knew with absolute certainty the year in which the book of Jonah was written, it would not prove that the author was the first or the only Jew who possessed a consciousness that his nation had responsibilities towards other nations. Indeed if his teaching had found *no* response, it would probably

THE SERVANT OF THE LORD 27

have perished utterly. But we are justified in saying that the circumstances of the time of Alexander the Great made it possible for Israel to have a wider, more liberal outlook than, humanly speaking, was possible in the days of Persian rule, or at any earlier period. Inasmuch as the book of Jonah appears to have been, for some time, part of the Canon in the days of Ben Sira, *i.e. c.* 200 to 180 B.C., it may therefore be presumed to have been in existence, at any rate, in the middle of the third century B.C., so that the *terminus ad quem* for the date of its composition must fall at all events within the generation following the death of Alexander. But since the book would appear to have been written in a time of peace, it is probable that the *terminus ad quem* is not later than the death of Alexander.

That the third century B.C., notwithstanding that upon the whole the lot of the Jews under the Ptolemies was far superior to what it had been under the Persians, was not a period favourable for the development among the Jews of a liberal sentiment towards the Gentiles is made probable from the use, which we find in some of the Psalms, of the name Rahab to denote Egypt. In Job ix. 13,

xxvi. 12, Rahab appears to be the name of the dragon power of the abyss, the *Tiamat* of the Babylonian Creation story. That the power of darkness should be taken as a symbol of the power of the Gentile world opposed to the people of God was natural enough ; and when Egypt was the Gentile power to which the Jews were compelled to pay tribute, tribute that was collected by such people as the sons of Tobias, it is not to be wondered at, if Egypt seemed to the Jews to be the embodiment of all that was opposed to their God, and that they applied to it the name of *Rahab*. But though the idea of Israel's obligation to the Gentile world had received a rough check, it was not destroyed, and was destined in happier times to develop and grow to the good of the world.

LECTURE II

It would naturally be of the greatest help to us in the study of those passages of the book of Isaiah which refer to the 'Servant of the Lord,' if we might assume the arrangement of the prophecies in the book to correspond with the order of their composition. Unfortunately this is impossible; for chapters, which at first sight might be regarded as homogeneous, are frequently found on a closer examination to consist of fragments having no logical connection with one another, the dates of which can only be determined by discovering the historical circumstances to which they are suitable. But although, if we find that every word in a prophecy of some length suits the known circumstances of some definite period and is unsuitable in any other, we may reasonably infer that it was composed at that period, in the case of *fragments* we are frequently compelled to admit that the circumstances of more than one period would account for their composition. Let us suppose, for example, that we have a number of denunciations of idolatry; it is certainly reasonable to assign their composition to a time when the Jews were peculiarly liable to temptations to idolatry. Let us suppose, however, that we are acquainted with two quite distinct periods in each of which this temptation existed; obviously in a book which covers both these periods, it is possible, if we cannot depend on chronological order, to assign such denunciations of idolatry to either period or to both, and in the case of each one of these prophecies we have no means of deciding with absolute certainty which is the correct period. Nor will a strong similarity between two passages necessarily prove that they are from the same hand; for the second may be an imitation of the first, composed at quite a different date. Moreover, in the case of imitation the mere position of a passage in a book which is not arranged in chronological order will be insufficient in itself to show whether the passage in question is the original or the imitation. It will thus be seen that the higher criticism of the prophets resembles

THE SERVANT OF THE LORD 31

the higher criticism of the Synoptic Gospels ; with these additional difficulties, that in the case of a prophetical book we have to deal with *one* book instead of *three* more or less parallel, and that, instead of having to sort out documents belonging, at any rate, to one generation, we have to disentangle fragments the dates of which may be centuries apart. One criterion in critical analysis of the prophets is, indeed, to be found in the metrical form in which many prophecies are written. But though the student must always take this into consideration, it will frequently fail him just where it is most necessary. Thus there are . some passages, where the parallelism of certain clauses makes it practically certain that we are dealing with compositions which *originally* possessed a poetical form, which, however, in the existing condition of the text, it is impossible to reduce with certainty to any exact rhythmical scheme. In some cases this is doubtless due to mutilation of the text ; but in others it may well be that the poetical form, in which a prophecy was composed and circulated orally, had already been lost, when the prophecy was first committed to writing, and in such a case it is obviously vain to attempt to correct the text on the basis of metre.

In the main, therefore, we are dependent upon the subject-matter of a section for its date; and consequently, where there is no definite historical allusion, we have nothing to go by but the ideas about God and His relation to His people, the relation of Israel to the Gentiles, and the like. Obviously under such circumstances it is impossible to fix a date for a given section with anything more than a certain degree of *probability*; for it does not follow because a certain idea was prominent at some particular time, that no one had ever thought of it before. Inasmuch, however, as it is desirable for a clear understanding of those passages which deal with the Servant of the Lord, to know approximately the date at which they were composed, I will examine as briefly as possible the dates of the 'Servant' passages of the book of Isaiah, and of those sections which are associated with them.

Since most people will admit that in the chapters xl.-liii. there are some passages which refer to Cyrus, and were presumably written in his time, while some people will assign

THE SERVANT OF THE LORD 33

to this date by far the greater part of this section, it will be well for me to specify those passages which I myself am disposed to assign to a later date, and to give my reason for so doing.

In chap. xli. 8-20 we have a section which certainly has no direct connection with the preceding context. It is of particular interest for our purpose, for in it Jehovah is represented as saying, 'But thou, Israel, my servant Jacob whom I have chosen, the seed of Abraham who loved me,[1] thou whom I have taken hold of from the ends of the earth, and called thee from the corners thereof.' If this passage really belongs to the time of Cyrus, it is the earliest passage outside the Pentateuch (except Ezek. xxxiii. 24, where Abraham is mentioned as an example of blessing) in which Abraham is mentioned as the ancestor of Israel; for Micah vii. 20 is almost certainly post-exilic; and the words 'who redeemed Abraham' in Isaiah xxix. 22 are probably an interpolation, but it is difficult, if not impossible, to account for some of its phrases on the assumption of this date. What, for

[1] אֹהֲבִי not the irreverent 'my friend' of the English version.

example, is meant by the statement that Jehovah has taken Israel from the ends of the earth ? The language can scarcely refer to the call of Abraham from Ur of the Chaldees ; for, though in Isaiah v. 26 the Assyrians are said to be summoned from the 'end of the earth,' a description which would be applicable to the land of the Assyrians in the time of Isaiah, when the Jews had not yet come into contact with them, would scarcely be suitable to Babylonia, when that country was as familiar to the Jews as it was in the time of Cyrus ; certainly it is hard to suppose that a Jew *living in Babylonia* would have described it as 'the ends of the earth.' Moreover, due weight must be given to the fact that here we have the *plural*, not 'end' but 'ends.' The expression would be equally inapplicable to the Exodus from Egypt : it would, however, be perfectly suitable if applied to a return from the Dispersion. In vv. 11, 12 it is implied that there are a *number of adversaries* opposed to Israel, not simply the Chaldaean king ; *i.e.* the situation seems to be the same as we find in some of the latest sections of the prophetical books and in the Psalms. Though the language of

THE SERVANT OF THE LORD 35

v. 14 *may* have been used by an exilic prophet, yet the expression 'worm' as applied to Israel, implies that the Jews are treated with a contempt of which we have no evidence in the exile, and the language resembles that of Ps. xxii. 6, Job xxv. 6; *i.e.* the atmosphere seems to be that of some of the Psalms. Verse 15, though it may have been suggested by a combination of Micah iv. 13 with Isaiah xl. 4, has a somewhat different *nuance* from the latter passage; for whereas in xl. 4 the mountains are merely types of obstacles which are to be removed, here the language suggests rather that they are types of heathen opponents who are to be crushed; *i.e.* we have here a note of vengeance which is absent in chap. xl. The statement of v. 17, that 'the poor and needy are seeking water, and there is none,' does not seem particularly suitable to the exiles; and the present tense 'are seeking' is opposed to the supposition that we have a picture of the returning exiles suffering from lack of water on their journey home. There is no indication that the trees which are to be planted in the wilderness are to protect Israel on the return to Palestine; and the words may well refer to the transformation of the waterless land, *i.e.* the land of the heathen (cf. Pss. lxviii. 6, lxiii. 1), into a garden by the preaching of the religion of Jehovah. Chapter xlii. 1-7 is closely allied with the other poems on Jehovah's 'Servant,' and must be considered in connection with them. It is commonly supposed that the rest of the chapter, at any rate in the main, belongs to the time of Cyrus, but it is at least possible to assign it to a later date. Thus the language of v. 10 recalls that of the Psalms, especially those Psalms which there is good reason to consider late (cf. Pss. xxxiii. 3, xl. 3, xcvi. 1, xcviii. 1, cxliv. 9, cxlix. 1, and also, if we may accept the plausible correction 'Let the sea roar' for 'Ye that go down to the sea,' Ps. xcvi. 11, xcviii. 7). The reference to Kedar may be explained at a period much later than that of the exile (cf. chap. lx. 7, Ps. cxx. 5), and if Sela be a reference to the land of Edom, we may compare Ps. lx. 9, Ps. lxxxiii. 6. In vv. 13-15 Jehovah's vengeance is depicted in language which contrasts forcibly with the calm hopefulness of chap. xl. There only the obstacles to Israel's return were to be removed, but here it seems to be implied that

THE SERVANT OF THE LORD 37

Jehovah in His vengeance will devastate the lands of Israel's foes. The blind who are led by Jehovah in v. 16 are not necessarily the Babylonian exiles, nor are the idolaters who are mentioned in v. 17 necessarily the Babylonian idolaters; the more natural interpretation being that the Israelites who listen to Jehovah's word are favourably contrasted with those Israelites who have turned to idolatry. The rest of the chapter, from v. 18 to the end, has been so modified from its original form that it is difficult, if not impossible, to decide what the first author wrote. Certainly the chaotic jumble of persons which we find at present cannot be primitive. It is not impossible that v. 19 is a gloss upon v. 18, but it is certainly not easy to account for the insertion of such a gloss. For the phrase 'my servant' will upon this supposition be quoted from other 'Servant' passages such as xlii. 1, lii. 13; and since in these the 'Servant' is mentioned with all honour, it is difficult to see why a *glossator* should have applied this honourable title to the nation in a passage where it is declared to be blind and deaf. Verses 18-21 may be a collection of mutilated fragments arranged together by an editor in consequence of their containing, or seeming to contain, certain points of contact. Verse 18 may originally have implied no rebuke, but may have been an announcement to the blind and deaf that now they may see and hear; cf. xxxv. 5. Verse 19, which appears to form a stanza or couplet, is evidently very corrupt, and its present form is probably due to the efforts of a scribe, or perhaps of more than one scribe, to correct it. Unfortunately, it is impossible to decide who is the speaker, for, though the phrase 'my messenger' would imply that it is Jehovah, the mention of 'the Lord's Servant' in the latter part of the verse is incompatible with this. Similarly in v. 20 it is impossible to decide whether the verbs were originally plural or singular, third person or second. Perhaps, since the words 'servant' (or 'servants') and 'messengers' occur in parallelism in xliv. 26, where the reference is apparently to the prophets who foretold deliverance from captivity, this passage (xlii. 19) is based upon that reference by one who regarded thé whole nation of Israel as called to be 'servants and messengers.' If this is the case, v. 19 must

THE SERVANT OF THE LORD

be considered to be independent of the other 'Servant' passages. Since, however, the text may be reconstructed in several different ways, it is quite impossible to give any very definite interpretation. We can only say that the verse was apparently written by some one whose conception of 'the Servant of Jehovah' was quite different from that of the writers to whom we must assign xlii. 1-7, xlix. 1-12, l. 4-10, lii. 13-liii. It is equally difficult to decide about the original connection of xlii. 21. If it is a pious reflection by an editor, it must be confessed that the working of his mind as he arranged this passage is not very obvious. If the first word of v. 22 is correct, it must refer back to a previous mention of Israel or Jacob, such as may originally have stood in v. 19, which, moreover, seems to be implied by v. 24. Here for the first person 'we have sinned' the third person should probably be read. These latter verses *may* be the work of a prophet at the close of the exile (cf. Zechariah i. 4); but the insistence on Israel's sin, and the statement that the people are robbed and spoiled, snared in holes and hid in prison houses, a prey and a spoil, is scarcely suitable to the circumstances at the close of the exile, and seems to require an historical background similar rather to that which is indicated in Ps. xliv.

Chapter xliii. is usually assigned to the time of Cyrus, and some portions, for example v. 14, can scarcely refer to any other period. At the same time, it must be admitted that there are some phrases which would be equally suitable at a later date. In 'the waters' and 'the rivers' in v. 2 there is not necessarily any reference to the rivers through which Israel must pass on its way home from Babylon, as is shown by the mention of the fire and flame in the latter part of the verse. The expression is a proverbial one as in Ps. lxvi. 12. The mention of Egypt, Ethiopia, and Seba is plausibly explained by the expected conquest of these countries by Cyrus (for the thought cf. Ezekiel xxix. 19, 20); but v. 5 f. seems more suitable to a return from the Dispersion than from the Babylonian Exile. The chapter is almost certainly not homogeneous; there is no reason for supposing that v. 8 originally followed v. 7. Again in vv. 22-28 we have a section which has no connection with the preceding context, and of which the

THE SERVANT OF THE LORD 41

exact meaning is by no means clear. As the text stands, Jehovah seems to be complaining that Israel has been weary of serving Him, and has not troubled to offer sacrifices to Him, and we seem to have a rebuke similar to that contained in Malachi i. 6 ff. Some commentators, however, would emend the text to make it mean that Jehovah has not required Israel to bring sacrifices (because Israel is not in Jerusalem), and that Israel is therefore called upon to undergo no labour in connection with the service of Jehovah, while, on the other hand, Israel has wearied Jehovah with its sins. Inasmuch as we do not know the source of this section, it is impossible to decide with certainty as to its original meaning. It is not impossible that it presupposes the same situation as Ps. l. It is commonly supposed that xliv. 1 ff. is from the same hand which composed xliii. 27, 28. It is, however, remarkable that in v. 27 we have the statement that Israel's 'first father' (viz. Jacob) *sinned*, and that the subsequent history of the nation has been in accordance with the beginning, while in the very next verse Jacob is declared to be Jehovah's servant whom He will bless.

42 THE SERVANT OF THE LORD

Chapter xliv. is commonly regarded as belonging to the time of Cyrus, except that several recent commentators regard the section against idolatry, vv. 9-20, as a late insertion. It is, however, questionable whether vv. 1-8, 21-23 are from the hand which wrote xliv. 24 – xlv. 8. True, if we argue merely from the occurrence of certain phrases and from the general style, we can hardly refuse to admit the identity of authorship; for we have the phrase, 'Jacob my servant, and Israel whom I have chosen' in xliv. 1 (cf. 2, 21), while in xlv. 4 we read, 'For Jacob my servant's sake, and Israel my chosen'; moreover, in xliv. 2, 24 we have the phrase, 'That formed thee from the womb.' Yet apart from these resemblances in style which may be partly the result of imitation, partly due to editorial expansion,[1] it cannot be maintained that there is any great probability that xliv. 1-8, 21-23 were composed

---

[1] Thus it is by no means certain that the words in v. 24, 'thy redeemer and he that formed thee from the womb,' were originally part of this section. In fact vv. 24, 25 cohere very badly with v. 26; for though the transition from the first person to the third is natural where *general* truths are being stated, as in vv. 24, 25, it is unsuitable in 26, 27. Jehovah would not be represented as saying of Himself that He is *one who* saith to Cyrus!

THE SERVANT OF THE LORD 43

in the time of Cyrus, at any rate by a Babylonian Jew. If the word 'Jeshurun' is correct in v. 2, it is probable that we have a reference to the book of Deuteronomy (xxxii. 15, xxxiii. 5, 26), a probability which is strengthened by the use of the word 'Rock' in v. 8 (cf. Deut. xxxii. 18). Whatever views be held as to the date of Deuteronomy, few people will be disposed to date chapters xxxiii. and xxxiv. earlier than the exile, and it is difficult to suppose that a Babylonian Jew would quote a Palestinian document at this early date. There is nothing in the imagery of v. 3 which is particularly suitable to Babylonia, and v. 5 seems to be a reference to the conversion of the Gentiles, a thought which certainly did not come into *prominence* till later than the time of Cyrus. Verse 23, if it was written in Babylonia, must have been written by a man whose view of nature was based on his Palestinian recollections.

In xlv. 1-7 we have a section which we may confidently assign to the time of Cyrus, and which is important for our purpose, inasmuch as it contains the words, 'For Jacob my servant's sake, and Israel my chosen.' It is not, however, easy to determine how much more of the chapter should be assigned to this date. Verse 8 might have been written at this time, or later. The section vv. 9-13, though printed by the Revisers as one paragraph cannot be homogeneous, or, if homogeneous, cannot be complete. There is no antecedent to the pronoun in v. 13, which appears to be a misplaced fragment of a prophecy concerning Cyrus.

In xlv. 14 the reference to Egypt, Ethiopia, and Seba, though it may have been suggested by xliii. 3, has an entirely different meaning from that in the former passage. *There* Egypt, Ethiopia, and Seba were given to *Cyrus* as compensation for Israel (in much the same way that Ezekiel had promised Nebuchadnezzar Egypt as a compensation for that king's disappointment concerning Tyre); *here* the wealth of Egypt, Ethiopia, and the Sabeans is to belong to *Israel*, and they themselves are to be subject to Israel, and the thought is similar to that which we find in Ps. lxxii. As a matter of fact, a close examination of the short section vv. 14-17 will show how extraordinarily complex it is. It is very doubtful whether any of the verses of which it is composed originally stood in juxtaposition.

THE SERVANT OF THE LORD 45

Similarly in the section xlv. 18-25: the impression which we naturally derive from v. 19, is that we have a lesson addressed to *Israel*, not (as we must suppose if v. 20 be in its right context) that Jehovah's dealings with Jacob are mentioned simply to encourage the heathen to come to Him. Verses 24, 25, which mention Jehovah in the third person, cannot be part of a speech in which Jehovah speaks in the first person.

Chapter xlvi. may perhaps in the main refer to the time of Cyrus, though it has not come down to us in its original form, and it may be the work of more than one author. Verse 3 has been placed by an editor, who was perhaps himself the author of it, after v. 2, simply because it contains the words הָעֲמֻסִים and הַנְּשֻׂאִים, while the preceding section has נְשֻׂאֹתֵיכֶם עֲמוּסוֹת מַשָּׂא; and similarly the section 6-7, which has itself suffered some mutilation, is placed after v. 4 because it contains the roots סבל and נשׂא which are found in v. 4. This method of arrangement, according to the use of similar phrases, is also found in the Psalter.

Chapter xlvi. 9-11 probably belongs to the time of Cyrus, though the text of v. 11 is not above suspicion; vv. 12, 13 may well be later. Of the date of chapter xlvii there can happily be no doubt, as it is a poem celebrating the downfall of the Chaldaean empire. We are not, however, obliged to assign its composition to the same prophet as chapter xl. 1 ff., unless we are convinced that Israel, the nation of prophets, only produced one prophet at that crisis.

Chapter xlviii. is composed of fragments: vv. 1 and 2 apparently are part of a denunciation of Jews who are unworthy of their privileges; but even here there must be a hiatus, for *in form* verse 2 gives the reason for the statement in verse 1 that the people swear falsely, and this is obviously impossible; people do not swear falsely *because* they are called after the Holy City. Verse 3 is a fragment of, or a quotation from, the words of the prophet of the Babylonian exile, who is commonly called the 'Deutero-Isaiah'; vv. 4, 5 are addressed to Israel in the *singular*; v. 6 is corrupt, but is perhaps from the same source as v. 3, and so probably is v. 7, except the last clause which reminds us of v. 5; v. 8 seems to be a continuation of the rebuke in 4, 5, and likewise v. 9; v. 10 is part of a

THE SERVANT OF THE LORD 47

declaration by Jehovah that He has smelted Israel in the furnace of affliction, and must therefore belong to a time when the faithful had been made evident by a time of affliction ; v. 11 is a statement by Jehovah that He will vindicate His name, which would be suitable in various contexts ; vv. 12-15, though not free from corruptions, evidently refer to the time of Cyrus ; v. 16 is a mutilated fragment in the beginning of which Jehovah is the speaker, and in the latter part the prophet ; vv. 17-19 are apparently a lament over Israel's disobedience belonging apparently to the age of the glorification of the Law ; v. 20 seems to be an exhortation to the Jews to flee by stealth from Babylon before the city be overwhelmed ; v. 21, which has no immediate connection with the preceding verse, is apparently part of an exhortation to Israel to remember how Jehovah led His people, and provided for them in the wilderness ; v. 22 seems to be a reflection on v. 19, which is taken from lvii. 21.

In chapter xlix. 1-6 we have a poem in which Jehovah's ' Servant ' describes his call and destiny, and in vv. 7-12 we have a section (if indeed it be homogeneous), based upon various passages in this book (*e.g.* xli. 18, li. 7, 12, liii. 3, xl. 1, 3, 4, xli. 17. Verses 14-26 is a section, mutilated in places, and perhaps not homogeneous, describing the restoration of Jerusalem, and the return of the Jews from the dispersion, who are to be carried back in triumph to their home by the Gentiles who have ceased to oppress them. Probably no portion of this section is as early as the exile ; for v. 17 implies that those who have destroyed Jerusalem are *at present in Jerusalem*. The idea of v. 20 is perhaps taken from Zech. ii. 4. Verse 26 reminds us of Zechariah ix. 15.

Chapter l. 1-3 has affinities with many late passages, and is itself probably late.

Chapter l. 4-9 is a soliloquy of the ' Servant ' describing his sufferings and looking forward to his triumph, verses 10, 11 being an appendix.

In chapter li. 1-6 we have a couple of fragment (viz. 1-3, 4-6). The lateness of the first is clear from v. 3, where there is a distinct reference to Isaiah xl. by a prophet who thought that that prophecy had now been fulfilled. The fact that it had already in his time been understood figuratively, and not of the return of the exiles from Babylon

THE SERVANT OF THE LORD 49

through the wilderness is plain, for we have a *desert* (*araba*) assigned to Sion! Verses 4-6 are either based upon xlvi. 12 or are from the same hand. Verses 7, 8 contain a somewhat similar appeal. It is noticeable that the appeal is not addressed to Israel as a whole, but to 'those who know righteousness.' Verses 9, 10 recall the language of Ps. lxxiv; v. 11 has been added by an editor or scribe from xxxv. 10, where it coheres better with the context. The word 'redeemed' was the cue which caused the addition. Verses 13-15 are an appeal to Israel to keep faith in Jehovah at a time of *persecution*, therefore not in the time of Cyrus. In vv. 17-23, Jerusalem, which is represented as stupefied with her afflictions, is bidden to arouse herself from her stupor, inasmuch as Jehovah is giving to those who have afflicted her the cup which she has drunk.

Chapter lii. 1, 2 are a declaration addressed to Zion, perhaps by the same writer as li. 17, but apparently at a somewhat later date, that the time of humiliation is over, and that there shall no more enter again into the holy city the 'uncircumcised and the unclean.' Verse 3 has no immediate connection with the preceding or following context: for the thought cf. Ps. xliv. 12. Verse 4 is fragmentary and the exact reference is uncertain. Verse 5 declares that Jehovah's people have been taken away from Him by heathen. The thought is not that of the exile, but of a later period. In vv. 7-10 we have a prophecy of comfort evidently based upon Isaiah xl., but containing a thought which is not found there, but is prominent in the Psalms, viz. that Jehovah is King. Verses 11, 12 are apparently an adaptation of an exhortation resembling that in xlviii. 20 to the exigencies of a later time. It is, however, impossible to speak with certainty, for the verse is not in its original context, since there is no antecedent to the pronoun 'her' in v. 11. Verse 12 would seem to be appended later. The language is based upon the story of the Exodus and conquest of Canaan.

It is therefore clear that we have in the chapters which I have thus briefly analysed a collection of *fragments* arranged with very little regard to their original connection. Of these the nucleus would appear to be the prophecies of one, or possibly more than one, prophet of the time of Cyrus, which from their great beauty, and from the brilliancy of their faith powerfully impressed later prophets. If, however, the foregoing analysis is in the main correct, there is a difference of tone between the original prophecies and those which at a later date were founded upon them. The former are almost unmixed consolation and encouragement; the latter exhibit a full recognition of the fact that the troubles which have come upon Israel are the result of Israel's sin.

Of the nucleus of this collection of prophecies, the analysis of which we have considered, the most important portion for our purpose is the section Isaiah xlv. 1-7; for here, not only in a passage which mentions Cyrus, but in a verse which can scarcely be addressed to any one else, we find the phrase, 'For Jacob my servant's sake, and Israel my chosen'; and we may therefore conclude with tolerable certainty that, at a date not later than 538 B.C., a prophet spoke of his nation as being in some sort the 'servant' and the 'chosen' of Jehovah. We naturally ask, therefore, what ideas he connected with these words. Is there here any thought of a mission for Israel?

52 THE SERVANT OF THE LORD

Now it may be stated as a characteristic of Hebrew style generally, that we never find expressed by means of an *adjective* or *adjectival clause* an idea which is not necessary for the understanding of the main sentence. If, therefore, the words ' chosen ' and ' servant ' implied a choice in order to fulfil some special mission, we should expect to find in the immediate context an account of this mission. In the passage before us the whole stress is laid upon the mission of *Cyrus*, and it would, therefore, be contrary to Hebrew idiom to refer *by the way* to a mission of Israel. The words, ' my servant ' and ' my chosen,' which, of course, refer to Israel, must therefore be used simply to explain the *mission of Cyrus*. In other words, Jehovah has given Cyrus the victory for the sake of His people Israel, who stand to Him in a special relation, viz. that of servant. Israel is thought of as one who is, so to speak, attached to the household of Jehovah ; one who stands in the same relation to Jehovah as a courtier, who not only has free access to a king, but receives the *special protection* of the king. This is apparently the sense which the word has, when it is used, for example, of Abraham

THE SERVANT OF THE LORD 53

in Gen. xxvi. 24, of Jacob in Ezekiel xxviii. 25, xxxvii. 25, of Zerubbabel in Haggai ii. 23, of the 'Branch' in Zechariah iii. 8. There is, however, an advance from the thought in the passages quoted from Genesis and Ezekiel, in that phrases used there of the individual patriarchs are here used of the nation. The phrase 'my chosen' receives illustration from Zechariah i. 17, ii. 12. It means what Amos means by the words, 'You only have I known of all the families of the earth.'

We may say then that, before the end of the sixth century B.C., Israel as a whole was spoken of as the 'Servant of Jehovah'; the phrase meaning primarily that Israel in a special sense enjoyed the favour and protection of Jehovah. But a phrase which has once become current may in course of time suggest a conception somewhat different from that which it bore in the mind of its originator. We may, perhaps, see a trace of the transition in Malachi i. 6, although Malachi in this passage is thinking of the priests, and not of the whole nation. 'A son honoureth his father, and a servant his master,' says Malachi: 'if then I be a father, where is mine honour? and if I be a master, where is my fear? saith the Lord of hosts unto you, O priests that despise my name.' Here the prophet is thinking of the obedience that is due to Jehovah and the work which should be conscientiously performed for Him, not of the protection which a king affords his servants. It is not unlikely that this aspect of service, which Malachi impresses upon the priests, was constantly brought before the Jews in the age following Nehemiah's publication of the Law, and that the Jewish Church, or at least the better portion of it, considered that Jehovah had made Israel His servant in order that Israel might faithfully carry out His commands.

It is improbable that during the Persian period the nation ever supposed that Jehovah had commanded, or would command, His servant Israel to preach His Law to the Gentiles; for the policy of Nehemiah had been to isolate Israel from the Gentiles; but if the assignment of the book of Jonah to the time of Alexander the Great is correct, we may conclude that by that time at least a section of the Church had perceived, however dimly, that what the prophets had been in Israel, that Israel ought to be in the world.

THE SERVANT OF THE LORD 55

But the hopes which had been raised by the conquests of Alexander were destined for a time to be shattered. Before the close of the fourth century B.C. the Jews found themselves beneath the yoke of the Ptolemies, which they bore till 198 B.C.; and although there can be little doubt that their position had enormously improved from what it had been in the days of Persian rule, the thought of paying tribute to Egypt was particularly galling to them, at least to the non-Hellenising section of the people. The wider outlook which we find in the book of Jonah would, therefore, be likely to give way to some extent to the exclusiveness of Nehemiah.

And meanwhile there was a gradually widening rift in Judaism. On the one hand, there were those who welcomed the civilisation which the Macedonian conquest had brought with it, and on the other, there were those who regarded every departure from the old customs, whether good or bad, as virtually apostasy from Jehovah. No doubt, among those who in the third century would have been described by the more conservative party as Hellenisers, there were some who were generally loyal to the Law of their fathers;

but since, as a rule, it must have been profitable to stand well with the ruling classes, the ranks of the Hellenisers would naturally contain many who cared nothing about real religion, and were only anxious for worldly advantage. In the eyes of these latter those who clung so tenaciously to the Law of their fathers (who belonged for the most parts to the poorer ranks of society, and to the country rather than to the town) were a set of hopelessly unreasonable fanatics exciting the contempt of reasonable men, whose opinion might be entirely disregarded. Accordingly, while the upper classes cultivated Greek ways, the poorer classes, isolated more and more from their wealthier brethren, tended to become what was virtually a Church apart. They worshipped, indeed, at Jerusalem, and acknowledged the authority of the priests who there ministered, but it seemed to them that of the Jewish nation only a small portion, and that the poorest and weakest portion, could claim in any way to fulfil the purpose for which Jehovah had chosen Israel. It was, speaking generally, only the *poor* who could with any propriety be described as a people for Jehovah's own possession.

THE SERVANT OF THE LORD 57

By the time of Antiochus Epiphanes these opponents of Hellenism had come to be called by a distinctive name, viz. *Hasîdîm*, or, in the Aramaic form which underlies the spelling of the Greek word found in the first book of Maccabees, *Hasîdayyâ*. The name *Hāsîd*, of course, denotes one who is in some way or other an example of *hesed*. It is not, however, easy to decide exactly what it connoted; whether those who bore the name laid stress on kindness to the poor (in which some of the wealthy Hellenisers were terribly deficient), or whether they were simply the religious as distinct from the irreligious. On the whole, the former is perhaps the more probable view, especially as at this period great stress was laid on the duty of almsgiving. It is impossible to say whether the name Hasîdîm was given by the Hellenisers in mockery, or whether it was taken as the party name by those who bore it. Whatever its origin was, however, the Hasîdîm came to regard it as an honourable title.

One element in Jewish religious life in the third and second centuries before Christ must not be forgotten, viz. the existence of synagogues, which are probably mentioned in Ps. lxxiv. 8. Since the priests formed to a great extent the aristocracy of Judaism, and the aristocracy were most strongly influenced by Hellenism, it is likely that the Temple offered no rallying point to those who were zealous for the faith of their fathers. With the synagogues, however, it was different. If, as is probable, the synagogues had had their origin in a desire for instruction in the law, it is obvious that the Hellenisers would not have any affection for them. It was one thing to go through official worship at the Temple ; it was another to spend time in the study of laws, many of which they regarded as barbarous and obsolete. It is extremely probable, therefore, that if we could have gone into a Jewish synagogue in the first quarter of the second century before Christ, we should have found ourselves in a congregation composed entirely of Hasîdîm. Those who worshipped in synagogues would thus have formed, to all intents and purposes, a community apart. The Temple was a place in which to *sacrifice*, and, save that its ritual differed from that of Gentile temples, there was nothing (with the possible exception of certain hymns sung by the Levitical choirs)

THE SERVANT OF THE LORD

to remind the Jew that he belonged to a nation apart. In the synagogue, however, he received instruction in the unique Law of Israel; in the synagogue he heard read the sacred books which related what great things Jehovah had done for his fathers; in the synagogue he could never forget that he was a Jew, of the seed of Jacob, a fact of which the Hellenisers appeared to have lost sight; and consequently he would naturally be disposed to regard those who attended the synagogues as the true Israel, the true heirs to the promises which Jehovah had made to the fathers, the true remnant of Israel which in the end would be saved.

LECTURE III

I HAVE already endeavoured to trace out the development in Israel of a consciousness of Jehovah's choice of the nation to be His servant; and, in order to do this, it has been necessary to analyse briefly the group of chapters which contain references to the 'Servant of the Lord.' It is now necessary, in order to carry forward our study, to consider more closely the passages which refer specially to this 'Servant.' Of these the most important are four which it is the fashion to speak of as 'Songs.' The term is not altogether a satisfactory one, for there is nothing to suggest that these four poems, or fragments of poems, were specially intended to be sung, any more than many other portions of the book. In one respect, however, it is useful, inasmuch as it suggests that these poems possess a *definite rhythmical form.* It is pretty generally agreed that these four passages possess a certain independence, and that, whatever be their origin, the position which they now occupy in the book is not that in which they were originally placed.

One thing may be said with tolerable certainty. The four passages, though they may not be altogether complete, and though the text of them has to some extent been corrupted, show in each case signs of literary unity. They are not mere comments, editorial additions to the context in which we now find them, but each of them was originally as distinct as, for example, one of the Psalms.

There is much that we cannot hope to discover. By whom they were composed, when and where they were first written down, —these are questions to which we cannot give any definite answer. We cannot even tell whether they existed in writing before they were incorporated in the book of Isaiah, though this is certainly probable. Considering the extraordinary abruptness with which they begin, without any introduction to show who is the speaker, it is reasonable to suppose that they are to be regarded as excerpts from some *collection of prophecies* dealing with the subject of 'Israel the Lord's Servant.' And although, if this be the case,

THE SERVANT OF THE LORD 63

it is difficult to understand why the editor of the book of Isaiah should have selected just these excerpts, and should have rejected their setting, a like editorial arbitrariness, if it be right to call it arbitrariness, is found elsewhere. Why, for example, should the section which we find in Isaiah ii. 2-4, Micah iv. 1-4 have been inserted in its present context ?

In these four passages we find a diversity of speakers. In the first (xlii. 1-4) the speaker is Jehovah; in the second (xlix. 1-6), and in the third (l. 4-9) the Servant Himself speaks; in the fourth (lii. 13-liii.), except in some instances where the text probably needs correction, we find the declaration of a number of people, that is to say, the verbs are in the first person plural.

I have already stated that the four passages which we are specially considering are *poems*, that is to say, they possess a definite rhythmical form; and inasmuch as it will be necessary in a discussion of the integrity of the text to take account of this, it will be well that I should describe briefly the ordinary laws of Hebrew poetry. It is, indeed, affirmed by many scholars that Hebrew poetry is governed by no fixed rules; and it may be freely admitted that in the case of a number of Psalms it is impossible either to arrange them as they stand according to any exact scheme, or to reconstruct the text in such a way as to reduce it to a precise poetical form. It such cases, as perhaps in the case of the New Testament canticles, it is probable that all that was aimed at was the production of a composition which could be sung to certain chants.

In a great number of cases, however, the evidence for a more or less exact poetical form is unmistakable. In my opinion a careful critical study of the book of Job, and of many of the Psalms, establishes this fact beyond question ; and although few poems, as they have come down to us, conform in all their parts to any rule, it is probable that, after making allowance for a certain amount of poetical licence, we should attribute this irregularity to corruption of the text. The Hebrew text which has come down to us would seem, in many places, to have been copied from mutilated manuscripts, or from manuscripts which were partly illegible. The scribes apparently copied what they could

THE SERVANT OF THE LORD 65

read without attempting to restore or complete the text. Happily, however, owing to one of the chief characteristics of Hebrew poetry, the general sense has been preserved in many places, even where there is good reason to suppose that the text is incomplete. Speaking generally, the most prominent characteristic of Hebrew poetry is *parallelism*, a balancing of clause by clause, and line by line. The poet makes a statement in a few words containing a certain number of rhythmic beats, and then completes the line by a parallel statement, whether nearly synonymous or antithetical, consisting of an equal number of beats.[1] Such a line is immediately followed by a parallel or complementary line of like construction, the two lines forming a couplet. A definite progress in the thought of the poem, or new idea, will be introduced in a new couplet. Thanks to this parallelism, the sense may remain almost unimpaired, though a whole line may be lost.

A good illustration of this poetical structure

[1] This is true of the ordinary hexameter or octameter rhythm, but not of the pentameter (*e.g.* Ps. xix. 7-10), in which the two beats which follow the *caesura* of each line are not parallel in sense to the three beats before it, but complementary.

is seen in the old poem in Micah vi. 6 ff., which is composed in Hexameter lines (*i.e.* lines of six beats with a *caesura* in the middle, the latter half being parallel to the first) arranged in couplets. The words which are the rendering of those on which the beat falls in the Hebrew are marked by an accent.

Wherewíth shall-I-méet Jehóvah,
  bów-myself tó-the-Gód of-heáven?
Sháll-I-meét-Him [1] with-burnt-ófferings?
  with-cálves of-a-yéar óld?
Will-He-be-pleásed with-thoúsands of-ráms,
  with myriads of-the-fat-pórtions of peace-ófferings?
Shall-I-gíve my-fírstborn as-my-transgréssion-offering,
  my-womb-fruit as my sin-óffering? [2]

In studying a Hebrew poem therefore the first thing to be discovered is whether any

[1] הַאֲקִדְּמֶנּוּ is to be regarded as two beats. Possibly the word should be pointed as Hiph'il. It seems to be a rule that a word which has two syllables long by nature in addition to the accented syllable may be scanned as two beats.

[2] Omit יהוה and read חֶלְבֵי שְׁלָמִים (as in 1 Kings viii. 64) for נַחֲלֵי שָׁמֶן.

Read חַטַּאת חֲטָאתִי for חַטַּאת נַפְשִׁי. Since בֶּטֶן, is perpetually simply a synonym of רֶחֶם, it is improbable that it is here used of the *father*. פְּרִי בִטְנִי is to be regarded as virtually a compound word 'womb-fruit,' the suffix pronoun defining the whole expression.

parts of it conform to the rules described above. If so, it may be assumed that the poem was originally written according to a definite poetical scheme, and since the rules of parallelism are as precise in their way as rules of rhyme in English poetry,[1] we shall have an invaluable means of testing the text as a whole, and often of making good deficiencies.

A useful illustration of poetical structure in Hebrew, and of the help which may be derived from this in the restoration of the

---

[1] No one would hesitate to admit the existence of corruption in an English rhymed poem of which some stanzas were only half the proper length and destitute of rhyme. Let it be supposed, for example, that the first stanza of the Old Hundredth occurred only in this form : ' All people that on earth do dwell, Come ye before Him and rejoice'; the second stanza being complete, no one would deny that we should be justified in arguing that the first stanza was mutilated. In this case we should be led to discover the exact nature of the corruption by observing that, although the line 'Come ye before Him,' etc., makes some sort of sense, if read immediately after the first line, yet there is no antecedent to the pronoun 'Him,' which requires some previous mention of the Lord. But if the line 'Come ye before Him,' etc., cannot be the original second line of the stanza, the absence of any rhyme between its last word and that of the first line makes it impossible that it can be the third. We should therefore conclude, quite correctly, that the missing lines were the second and third, though it would obviously pass the wit of man to say precisely what the missing words ought to be.

text may be found in Psalm ii. Since the first verse down to the words, 'take counsel together,' forms an exact hexameter couplet,[1] and the words, 'Let us break their bonds asunder, and cast away their cords from us,' form a complete hexameter line, it is reasonable to suppose that the psalm originally followed the ordinary hexameter rhythm. But no one who pays any attention to the laws of parallelism can read the psalm, as it stands, without being struck by the fact that the words, 'against the Lord and against His anointed,' have no parallel in the first part of the line, and further that the words, 'Let us break,' etc., are introduced without any indication of the speaker. It will also be noticed that the words, 'and against His anointed,' are naturally parallel to the words, 'against the Lord,' and we should therefore conclude that they belonged to a parallel *clause*; in other words, 'against the Lord' is the conclusion of the first half of a line, and 'against His anointed' the beginning of the second half.

With this clue we are able to gain some idea

[1] Some commentators, regarding each of the parallel clauses in one sentence as a line, speak of *quatrains*.

of the original form of the psalm, which we can arrange in couplets, thus :—

> Why do the Gentiles rage,
>> and the peoples imagine a vain-thing?
> the kings of the earth stand up,
>> and the rulers take counsel together?

The first couplet, which asks the reason for the excitement among the Gentiles, is thus complete. The second couplet will then develop still further the account of the Gentiles' hostility by stating what they design to do. We may make good the deficiency in the first line somewhat as follows :—

[They have said, We will contend] against Jehovah,
  and against His anointed [we will gather together to fight]:
we will break their bonds asunder,
  and cast away their ropes from us.

The next couplet describes the futility of all these schemes of revolt.

> He that dwelleth in heaven will laugh,
>> the Lord will have them in derision.
> Then will He speak unto them;
>> in His wrath and hot anger He will affright them.

Verse 6 f. formed originally two couplets, but the parallel line to v. 6 is lost, and one clause of the following couplet. We may arrange the verses thus:—

> While I (for my part) am constituted King,
>   yea, upon His holy hill of Zion.¹

Jehovah's anointed then goes on to develop the thought which is implied in the statement that he is constituted King in Zion.

> I will give an account of Jehovah's decree;
> He hath said, Thou art My son,²
>   I myself this very day have begotten thee.

The next couplet then describes the privileges of the anointed King who receives a share of territory from Jehovah who has adopted him as son. The words 'Desire of me and' are unnecessary to the sense; they destroy the rhythm, and are probably a later insertion. The couplet should run:—

> I will give the Gentiles for thine inheritance
>   and the ends of the earth for thy possession;
> thou shalt shepherd³ them with a rod of iron,
>   yea, thou shalt dash them in pieces like a potter's vessel.

---

¹ Reading on the basis of the LXX. וַאֲנִי נִסַּכְתִּי מֶלֶךְ עַל־צִיּוֹן הַר קָדְשׁוֹ.

² According to the existing text the first half of the second line is too long by one beat. The only word which can be dispensed with is אֵלַי, which may have been introduced by a copyist or may belong to the missing half line, having been transposed with אָמַר.

³ Reading with LXX. תִּרְעֵם.

THE SERVANT OF THE LORD 71

In the next couplet the anointed King addresses a solemn warning to those who rebel.

> And nów, O ye kíngs, be wise ;
>   be admónished, ye júdges of the eárth.
> Sérve Jehóvah with feár
>   and trémble before Hím,[1] with quáking.

The text of the last couplet is very doubtful, grammar, rhythm, and sense alike being at fault, at any rate in the first line. It appears to have emphasised the admonition to the Gentiles by pointing out the consequences of rebellion and the blessedness of submission.

If, as I hope, these illustrations are sufficient to demonstrate the existence in Hebrew of an exact poetical structure as well as the assistance which such a structure affords us in detecting, and to some extent correcting, corruptions of the text, I shall be pardoned for this digression, inasmuch as we shall now be in a better position to consider the poems relating to ' The Servant of the Lord,' of which the original poetical form appears to have been identical with that which I have described.

In the first passage (Isaiah xlii. 1-4) it is not quite clear whether we have a description

---

[1] This seems to be the sense required, but the text is probably corrupt.

of Jehovah's Servant *as he actually exists*, or *an ideal* of what such a servant should be. Verse 3 in the Masoretic text somewhat favours the latter alternative, but there is good reason here for doubting the correctness of the text.

The opening words of this passage imply that the writer was familiar with the prophecies which had been uttered concerning Cyrus, and that he adapts the phrases which his great predecessor had originated, in order to set forth his view of the Servant of Jehovah. Thus the terms 'my servant,' 'my chosen,' appear to be taken from Isaiah xlv. 4; the phrase, 'whom I uphold,' may have been suggested by the words used of Cyrus in xlv. 1, though the verb there used is different, what seems to be a reminiscence of both passages being found in xli. 9; the words, ' I have put my spirit upon him,' *may* be borrowed from lxi. 1, but it is possible that in both cases the phrase is taken from the older Scriptures, as, for example, the story of the anointing of Saul or the commission of Elijah. The Septuagint inserts in the first two clauses the names Jacob and Israel; but inasmuch as the first verse forms a perfect couplet, each line consisting of two parallel clauses of three

THE SERVANT OF THE LORD 73

beats each, and inasmuch as the symmetry of the rhythm is spoilt by their insertion, in all probability the Masoretic text is here correct. The whole couplet, therefore, will run as follows :—

> Behold my servant, whom I uphold ;
> my chosen, in whom my soul delighteth :
> I have put my spirit upon him :
> he shall bring forth judgment to the Gentiles.

Verse 2 appears to be mutilated, as we have only one line instead of a whole couplet. It describes, or rather *did* describe, the mute patience of the Servant, who suffers uncomplainingly. This is somewhat obscured in the English version, where the words, 'He shall not cry,' seem to imply that the Servant's *preaching* will be done quietly. The Hebrew, however, implies rather, ' He will not cry for help.' The first line of the couplet, therefore, should be translated :—

> He will not cry for help, nor lift up his voice,
> nor cause his voice to be heard in the street.

The second line of the couplet is gone, but it must have been more or less parallel in thought to the first line, and no doubt expressed the same thought which is found in liii. 7.

Verse 3, *as it stands*, expresses the patience of the Servant in dealing with the weak, but

74 THE SERVANT OF THE LORD

since in v. 4 it is evident that it is the Servant himself who is, in accordance with the metaphors used, in danger of being extinguished or crushed, it is almost certain that we should read in v. 3 :—

> A bruised reed will *I* not break,
>   and a dimly-burning wick *I* will not extinguish.[1]

The parallel line has lost one of its clauses; it probably was somewhat to this effect :—

> For he shall proclaim my [law in the land];
>   to the coastlands he shall publish my justice.[2]

Verse 4 will then be a reiteration of what is affirmed in v. 3. One clause is gone, and another has suffered a slight corruption. We should probably read somewhat as follows :—

> For [Israel my chosen] will not burn dimly,
>   nor will [Jacob my servant] be crushed.[3]
> He will set judgement in the land,
>   and the coastlands will wait for his teaching.

The following verses, 5-7, are an appendix, but whether they were appended to the prophecy which they follow before or after the insertion of that prophecy in its present place it would be impossible to say. These appended verses, no less than the passage to

---

[1] *i.e.* reading אֲשַׁבּוֹר and אֲכַבֶּנָּה.

[2] Reading לְאִיִּים for לֶאֱמֶת and מִשְׁפָּטִי.

[3] Reading יִשְׂרָאֵל בְּחִירִי לֹא יִכְהֶה וְלֹא יָרוּץ יַעֲקֹב עַבְדִּי.

THE SERVANT OF THE LORD

which they are added, appear to have been composed by one whose inspiration was drawn both from the 'Cyrus' passages and from the 'Servant' passages (cf. for example v. 6 with xlix. 6 and 8). In v. 6 the tenses should probably be read as *past*, *i.e.* we should translate : ' I the Lord have called thee in righteousness, and I have grasped thine hand, and I have kept thee and have made thee a national covenant' (*i.e.* the mediator of a national covenant), ' for a light of the Gentiles ; to open the blind eyes to bring out the prisoners from the dungeon, and them that sit in darkness out of the prison house.' Here we have almost certainly a reminiscence of lxi. 1-3 as well as of xlv. 1. The conviction is expressed that the Servant has been called, not only to be the mediator of a *national* covenant (*i.e.* a covenant of Jehovah with His people Israel), but also to be a 'light to lighten the Gentiles.' There is obviously very little difference, if any, in the standpoint from which verses 1-4 were written and that from which the appended verses were composed. One may, perhaps, infer that the affliction of the Servant which appears to be still present in vv. 1-4 is a thing of the past in the appendix, but the language is scarcely conclusive on this point.

In the next passage, Isaiah xlix. 1-6, although the general sense is similar to that of the section which we have just considered, a more hopeful, more triumphant note is struck. Here the sufferings of the Servant, which are only hinted at, are clearly past; and the Servant is no longer mute in the midst of his afflictions, but lifts up his voice to the whole world in strong assurance that he has received from Jehovah not only a commission to be a light to the Gentiles (that is to proclaim to the Gentiles the teaching which goes forth from Sion, and the word of the Lord which goes forth from Jerusalem), but also power to make that mission a success. In chapter xlii. the Servant was presented to us uncomplaining in his weakness; here we see him rejoicing in his strength.

Now, as I have before pointed out, the Servant in this passage is distinctly stated (v. 3) to be Israel, and even though the name should here be supposed to be a gloss, the resemblance between this passage and xliv. 1 f. shows that is at any rate a correct gloss. The passage just referred to (xliv. 1) is

THE SERVANT OF THE LORD 77

important as showing that the words, 'The Lord hath called me from the womb; from my mother's body hath he made mention of my name,' do not necessarily imply that the speaker is an *individual* man. The Hebrews carried personification to a point where our prosaic western minds find it hard to follow them. Those who in ordinary *prose* could write of *tribes*, ' And Judah said unto Simeon his brother, Come up with me into my lot, that we may fight against the Canaanites; and I likewise will go with thee into thy lot' (Judges i. 3), could obviously in poetry go still further in the way of personification. As a matter of fact, the books of the prophets contain many examples of the application to Israel of language which is apparently suitable only to an individual. As an illustration it will be sufficient to mention Hosea xi. 1, 'When Israel *was a child*, then I began to love him.'

The Servant of Jehovah, therefore, who in this passage (v. 3) is represented as possessing in some way or other the right to be styled Israel, here claims that from the very beginning of his history Jehovah has destined him for a mission the glory of which has now been revealed to him. The Lord can select an

78 THE SERVANT OF THE LORD

individual or a nation as a vessel for His use, whether to honour or to dishonour. As He can make Ephraim His helmet, Judah His sceptre, and Moab His washpot, so He can make His Servant, whom He declares to be the true Israel, a sharp sword or a polished arrow. By the statement that Jehovah has made his mouth like a sharp sword, the Servant means that Jehovah has put into his mouth teaching which will overcome the wickedness of the world, as a warrior armed with a sharp sword overcomes his enemies. The thought is very similar to that which we find in chapter xi. 4, where it is said of the ideal ruler who will restore the throne of David that 'he will smite the violent (read עָרִיץ) with the rod of his mouth, and with the breath of his lips will he slay the wicked.' Jehovah has protected His Servant as a warrior guards his weapons, and has encouraged him by reminding him that he is *His* Servant: one, that is to say, whom He, Jehovah, will not allow to be unavenged, one, moreover, in whom will be manifested His glorious might.

The Servant has, however, in time past found it difficult to keep his faith in Jehovah

THE SERVANT OF THE LORD 79

and in his mission. In his afflictions it was hard to make his sense of God's justice square with his experiences. He then said, as other sorely tried servants of God have said, 'I have laboured in vain, I have spent my strength for nought and vanity: yet surely my cause must be with the Lord, and my recompense with my God' (v. 4). But, though it was once difficult to retain a belief in a mission, *now* the darkness is past, and a more glorious destiny is revealed than had previously been imagined. Now the Servant perceives that the scope of his mission is not Israel only, but the Gentiles also to the ends of the earth. Now that his God has become his strength (*i.e.* now that God has visibly made him strong, and has given him the victory), the restoration of Israel, which once seemed the most glorious of achievements, appears insignificant compared with the prospect of world-wide influence which now opens out before him (vv. 5, 6).

In verse 7 we come upon an appendix to the passage which we have just been considering, evidently containing reminiscences of the great prophecy in chapter liii. as well as of earlier prophecies. I have already called attention to the fact that it has phrases in common with the appendix to xlii. 1-4.

In the next passage, l. 4-9, the speaker is not specified, but he is obviously the same as in xlix. 1-6 ; and that he was regarded by the editor of the book as being the Servant of Jehovah is made probable by the fact that following upon this section comes the question, 'Who is among you that feareth the Lord, that obeyeth the voice of his servant ?' (v. 10). This speech, however, is spoken by the Servant not as in xlix. 1-6, when his triumph is manifest, but in the days of his conflict, when his ultimate triumph is still a matter of faith.

Unfortunately the opening verse is corrupt, though the general sense is fairly clear. The Servant declares that Jehovah has disciplined him, and that he has been an apt and obedient disciple. Jehovah has given him a well-trained tongue (lit. a tongue of disciples); that is to say, he has learned to repeat faithfully the message which has been entrusted to him ; while his ear has been rendered quick to catch the words which Jehovah speaks to him (v. 4). He has been called upon to undergo a discipline from which most people

THE SERVANT OF THE LORD 81

would have shrunk (v. 5) ; he has been exposed to persecution, and has been treated with contumely ; he has given his back to the smiters, and his cheeks to them that have plucked off the hair ; he has not refused to suffer shame and spitting (v. 6). For all the while he has been supported by his faith in Jehovah ; possessing a full assurance of the help, which in His own good time Jehovah will give, he has never been confounded. Knowing that he will not in the end be disappointed, he has set his face like a flint (v. 7). The Lord, who can and will vindicate him, is with him ; who then can oppose him ? who by overthrowing him can prove that he is one forsaken by the Lord (v. 8 f.) ?

In the fourth passage we are confronted with serious textual difficulties, though happily for the most part the general sense is clear. A full discussion of these difficulties is impossible without reference to the original Hebrew ; I will, however, endeavour to confine myself to those points which may be considered by those who are dependent upon the English versions.

In the first place we naturally ask whether the modern division of the text, which regards

vv. 13, 14, 15 of chapter lii. as forming one composition with chapter liii., is correct. Certainly it must be admitted that *prima facie* the division of our Bibles, which separates these portions by beginning a new chapter with the words, 'Who hath believed?' has much to recommend it. For, as the text stands, the speaker in lii. 13 can be none other than Jehovah; whereas in chapter liii. we have a plurality of speakers who acknowledge that the sufferings of the Servant have been in some way or other the consequence of their sin, and Jehovah is spoken of in the third person. The first person singular appears again according to the existing text in vv. 11, 12 of chapter liii. Apart from this difficulty, however, it must be admitted that chapter liii. appears to be the natural sequence of lii. 14; moreover, it is plain that liii. 1 can scarcely have been the *beginning* of the section.

But if lii. 13-15 is the beginning of a section of which chapter liii. is the continuation, it is obvious that the text of v. 13 has not come down to us in its original form; for the first person singular is evidently out of place. This, however, is not the only instance of corruption in the text. It is pretty obvious

THE SERVANT OF THE LORD

from chapter liii. that the section was originally a *poem* composed in the most common form of Hebrew poetry which I have already described, viz. in couplets of which each line consists of two parallel clauses. But it is impossible to reduce vv. 13 and 14 to couplets as they stand. Evidently we have here an example of that most common form of corruption in the text of the Old Testament, viz. the *omission of a number of words*, possibly through the scribe's eye having wandered, but more probably through the *mutilation of the manuscript* which he was copying. Now v. 13 ought to form a complete couplet, whereas at present we have only two not very exact parallel clauses of unequal length. Obviously it is impossible to restore the actual words which have gone, but from what remains we may assume that the opening couplet ran originally somewhat as follows :—

> Behold the servant of [Jehovah,
>   His chosen in whom He is well pleased],
> now shall he prosper, yea he shall be exalted,
>   and shall be lifted up and shall be very high.

The second couplet has lost the greater part of the second half of the first line, and has

84 THE SERVANT OF THE LORD

suffered also some minor corruptions, among them being the introduction of the second person instead of the third into the first clause, and the reading, 'so was a marring,' instead of 'for his countenance was marred.' The gist of the missing clause can be fairly well guessed from the context; and Psalm lxxxviii. will furnish us with clauses which would do very well as a makeshift. Probably the couplet ran originally somewhat as follows :—

> As they were appalled at [him,
>   and fled from him, even all] who saw him ; [1]
> for his aspect was marred that it was not that of a man,
>   and his visage that it was not that of a human being;

The next couplet will then describe the contrast to the Servant's condition of weakness and degradation described in v. 14. With the exception of the word (unwarrantably) translated 'He shall sprinkle,' which with the addition of one letter gives the more probable reading, 'shall see him,' the text here seems to have come down to us substantially as it left the author's hand. The couplet should probably read :—

---

[1] רבים is perhaps a blunder for רֹאָיו.

so shall many nations behold him,
> yea at him will kings shut their mouths;
for that which was not told them they have seen,
> and on that which they had heard not they have gazed.

The next couplet, of which, however, the last half is missing, develops the thought of the *unexpectedness* of the Servant's triumph. The pronoun 'our' is, however, unsuitable, for those who speak had been incredulous, and had not published any message. The omission of one letter would give the sense '*his* report,' viz. the preaching or message of the Servant; the objection to this, the simplest correction, is that in the parallel clause the reference is not to the Servant but to Jehovah, and the first clause needs another word to improve the rhythm. Perhaps therefore, with a slight rearrangement of the words, we may read :—

> Who believed Jehovah's message?
> > and His arm to whom was it revealed?

Since the next couplet begins with the word '*And* he grew up,' the missing line must have contained a reference to the Servant's obscure origin and weakness. We can bridge over the gap between v. 1 and v. 2 by supplying some such line as this :—

> [For His servant was poor and needy;
> > weak, and there was none to help him;]

In the following couplet (v. 3), by a very slight correction, we get the necessary sense, 'before *us*' instead of 'before *him*.' The text of the last clause also is in some confusion. We should probably render the verse thus :—

and he grew up before us as a sucker,
    and as a root from a dry ground ;
  (*Sc.* a shoot from the root of a cut-down tree, which everyone believes to be dead.)
he had no beauty nor majesty,
    and we saw him and desired him not.

In the next couplet, although the text of the first clause is somewhat uncertain, the uncertainty does not affect the verse as a whole, which may be rendered :—

He was despised and rejected of men,
    a man of sorrows and acquainted with sickness (or perhaps 'known by reason of sickness') ;
and, like one who hides his face from us,
    he was despised, and we esteemed him not.

The next couplet is contained in v. 4. It reads :

And yet it was our sicknesses that he bore,
    and our sorrows that he carried ;
but we esteemed him stricken,
    smitten of God and afflicted.

THE SERVANT OF THE LORD 87

The next couplet needs no correction. It runs :—

But he was wounded[1] through our transgressions,
    bruised (*or rather* crushed) through our iniquities ;
the chastisement of our peace (*or with a different pronunciation of the Hebrew*, The chastisement due to us) was upon him,
    and with his stripes we have been healed.

The next couplet (v. 6) is substantially correct, and in any case the sense is not affected. It reads :—

    All we like sheep went astray (cf. Ps. cxix. 176),
        we turned each one to his own way ;
    and Jehovah treated him as responsible,[2]
        [and made him bear][3] the guilt[4] of us all.

The next clause has been lengthened somewhat through the accidental repetition of a clause, and the word translated 'was dumb,' which should probably be masculine agreeing with the 'Servant,' has been misread as feminine agreeing with the sheep. The present state

[1] Cheyne questions this sense of the *Pô'al*, but it is more probable than the sense 'profaned.'

[2] I take this to be the meaning of the difficult word הִפְגִּיעַ.

[3] As another beat is necessary to complete the rhythm, it is probable that some such word as וַיַּסְבִּילֵהוּ has fallen out.

[4] That is, in accordance with a common Hebrew usage, the *consequences of guilt*, or what *appeared* to be such.

of the rhythm suggested that there may also be some other modifications of what was originally written. The corrected text will give the following couplet :—

> He was oppressed, yet he humbled himself,
>   [persecuted][1] yet opened not his mouth (cf. l. 6);
> as a lamb he was brought[2] to the slaughter (cf. Ps. xliv. 22 ; Zech. xi. 4);
>   and as a sheep before her shearers he was dumb.[3]

In the next couplet the text is in some confusion; perhaps the least change that is necessary to give sense is to read 'his judgment'[4] for 'and judgment he' (R.V.), and 'his way' (*i.e.* his fate) for 'his generation.'[5] We must also read 'our transgressions' for 'the transgression of my people,'[6] and 'he was smitten to death.'[7]

Of the following couplet, contained in v. 9, there is general agreement as to what must be the sense, though the Masoretic text is certainly not what the writer originally wrote.

---

[1] The rhythm shows that a word has fallen out.

[2] The tense shows that the verb is *frequentative*; cf. Ps. xliv. 22.

[3] Read נֶאֱלָם for נֶאֱלָמָה.   [4] *i.e.* מִשְׁפָּטוֹ for וּמִשְׁפָּט.

[5] *i.e.* דַּרְכּוֹ for דּוֹרוֹ, suggested by Cheyne.

[6] *i.e.* מִפְּשָׁעֵינוּ for מִפֶּשַׁע עַמִּי ; so Budde and Marti.

[7] So the LXX.

THE SERVANT OF THE LORD 89

Though 'poor' may sometimes denote the godly, we are not justified in saying that 'rich' was ever the equivalent of 'ungodly'; obviously we require two synonyms expressing the idea of wickedness. Instead of the word translated 'in his death' we require an expression parallel to the words, 'his grave was appointed'; perhaps we may venture to read, 'his corpse was cast forth' (cf. 1 Kings xiii. 24). The couplet will therefore have run somewhat as follows :—

> And his grave was appointed with transgressors,[1]
>   and with the wicked his corpse[2] was cast forth,
> although he had done no violence.
>   neither was any deceit in his mouth.

Verse 10 is hopelessly corrupt, and verse 11 is not much better. The last part of verse 10 is indeed translatable Hebrew; it is, however, impossible to accept it as the last line of a couplet, since the rhythm is wrong; we are therefore without any data for the restoration of the text. The sense of the English version, however, is probably so far

[1] So Cheyne and Marti.
[2] A not very violent alteration of the existing consonants would give בֵּית עוֹלָמוֹ, 'his long home' (cf. Eccles. xii. 5); but it is doubtful whether at this date such an expression could have been a mere synonym for *grave*.

correct that it represents the persecuted Servant as alive and prospering. Verse 11 is also corrupt past restoration, and it is impossible to say whether the word 'my Servant' is correct. If it is, the verse must be an *appendix* in which Jehovah is represented as speaking, and similarly also v. 12. Since, however, some such passage as this is necessary for the completion of the poem, and as v. 12 appears to have had originally the same poetical form as the other verses, we may probably in both verses account for the introduction of the first person by corruption of the text. The last couplet, therefore, should probably read somewhat as follows :—

> Therefore shall he have a share with the high,[1]
>   yea with the mighty shall he share the spoil ;
> forasmuch as he poured out his soul to death,
>   and with transgressors was numbered.[2]

Then follow some words which may be an editorial note or may be a fragment of another couplet: 'Now he bore the sin of many; and he interposes for the transgressors.'

---

[1] Read יְחַלֶּק־לוֹ and בְּרָמִים for בָּרַבִּים. The latter correction I owe to my former pupil, Mr. R. H. Willey.

[2] The rhythm here is halting, and the text is not above suspicion.

To sum up therefore, after making all allowance for textual corruption,[1] a good deal remains fairly certain. In the main the English version gives what is undoubtedly the general sense of the passage; though it is almost certainly wrong in representing the Servant in lii. 15 as a *priest* sprinkling many nations, and it is very doubtful whether in the original text liii. 10 contained any reference to an offering for sin, or v. 11 to any *future* justification of the many, and to the bearing of their iniquities. Upon the whole it is probable that a correct restoration of the corrupt verse, though it would, of course, bring out the beauty of the poem, and would make its meaning somewhat clearer, would not materially add to its sense.

What then do we learn from it as to the Servant of the Lord? Have we here a purely imaginary ideal picture? or a description of an actual fact? Is the author describing what he thinks will come to pass, or what he believes is already an accomplished fact?

[1] It is, of course, possible that some of the changes noted above from what the poet originally composed may have taken place in the course of the *oral transmission* of the poem. On the whole, however, it is more natural to regard them as due to imperfect manuscripts.

On this point it seems to me there is absolutely no room for doubt. A consideration of the tenses of the Hebrew verbs in this passage show conclusively that the author is here stating that the *Servant of the Lord has already been smitten to death*. He is describing an *historical fact*. There is, however, a reference to the future in the glorification of the Servant. It is evident that this glorification has begun, and that it is a cause of astonishment to those who have seen it; but it is to develop and grow still further.

In the next place we naturally inquire who are represented as speaking. Obviously they are those in whose midst and through whose fault the Servant of Jehovah has so grievously suffered. They once shunned him as one shuns a leper; they regarded him as one whom God had smitten, and treated him as though he were a criminal; yet now they recognise that the calamities which came upon him were the outcome, not of his wrong-doing, but of their own sins. They acknowledge that *they* went astray, and that their transgression and rebellion against Jehovah has not been visited upon them, but that all the consequence of it has come upon the

THE SERVANT OF THE LORD 93

Servant. He indeed was persecuted to the death ; nevertheless he lives ; he has achieved a victory in which they, who formerly held aloof from him and despised him, and through whose fault he suffered, have shared. They believe that henceforth he will be a power in the world.

Now, inasmuch as those who are represented as speaking in this great section mention Jehovah as one whose will has been made known to them, and inasmuch as there is no indication that they have recently turned to Him from idols, it may be regarded as unlikely that the heathen are intended. Had that been the case, we should almost certainly have had put into the mouth of the speakers a declaration that Jehovah is God alone. And since in other passages of this book where we find the first person plural, the reference is undoubtedly to Israel (cf. for example lix. 9 ff., lxiii. 16 ff.), we may safely conclude that in this place also those who speak are the Jewish nation.

LECTURE IV

WE have already seen that the passages which treat of the Servant of the Lord have many features in common; what is fully developed in one being at least implied in another. We may therefore take these passages together, and may consider the account of the Servant's career which is to be obtained by their combination.

The beginning of the Servant's career gave no promise of a brilliant future. He had no support from the influential; his own nation had scarcely recognised that he existed in its midst, and on his first appearance regarded him as contemptible. He was convinced, however, that he had received the teaching of the Lord, and he was an obedient and loyal disciple. But in following what he believed to be the Lord's commands, he encountered the fiercest opposition and obloquy; he was regarded as a pariah; he was made as the offscouring of the world;

he was persecuted and treated like a criminal; he was done to death, unresisting, as a sheep in the slaughter-house; he himself could not understand why the calamities should have come upon him; he was, however, steadfast in the conviction that he was Jehovah's Servant; he felt that Jehovah had recognised him as the true Israel, and that, in accordance with the promises made to the fathers, Jehovah would be glorified in him; though everything seemed hopeless, he was convinced that the Lord would help him; he felt that the restoration of the tribes of Israel, to which the prophets had looked forward, depended upon his steadfastness; he refused to give up this belief in his mission, and met death, still convinced that his cause would triumph; and when it seemed that his struggle had ended in utter failure, it was suddenly found to have been successful; though he had been done to death, he yet lived; his achievements filled with amazement those who had watched his career; even kings were astonished at his success; through his steadfastness in affliction he had won benefits not only for himself, but even for that section of his nation which had had no sympathy with him, and whose apostasy had been the cause of his sufferings; those who had once scoffed at him now accepted his teaching of Jehovah's will; the body politic of Israel had been sick indeed, but his struggle had brought healing; the Servant might be said to have already fulfilled to a great extent that which he himself believed to be his mission; he had raised up the tribes of Israel; but with this success his conception of his mission grew and developed; Gentile kings had been astonished at his achievements, and had been constrained to admit the might of Jehovah who had upheld him; therefore there now opened up a prospect of yet further influencing the Gentiles; Jehovah would make His Servant a light to the Gentiles, that all the earth might be partakers in the blessings which He had bestowed upon His people.

Whom then are we to understand by the Servant of Jehovah? In the first place are we to regard him as an individual, or as a personification of the nation or some section of the nation?

Against the supposition that an individual is intended by the Lord's Servant the evidence, in my opinion, is absolutely convincing. Not only is it extremely hard to believe that any Hebrew would ever have applied the name *Israel* to any individual man, even though he was the head of the nation, but there is a further objection which is quite insuperable. The Servant is described as actually suffering death and being buried among criminals; yet after all this he is represented as alive, and as going on from one success to another. I have already pointed out that the language of Isaiah liii. makes it quite certain that the career of the Servant there described is an accomplished fact. But it certainly could not have been said at any time in the history of the world before the resurrection of our Lord from the dead that an individual man who had been put to death, and had been buried, was still living, and triumphing, and advancing from one success to another.

But this, which could not be predicated of any individual man, could be affirmed of a nation, or of a section of a nation. When a Hebrew personified a multitude, it was not unnatural for him to assign to that multitude what in reality could only be affirmed of certain individuals composing it. Even in prose a Hebrew could write, 'And they (*sc.*

THE SERVANT OF THE LORD 99

the soldiers of the Assyrian army) awoke in the morning, and lo, they were all dead corpses.' Similarly the poet of Psalm xliv. says, 'For thy sake *are we killed all the day long*,' where of course the prose meaning is that continually members of that community, in whose name the poet speaks, are being put to death.

The natural interpretation, therefore, of the language used about the Servant is that a *plurality of persons is intended by the author*. We have still to decide, however, between the whole nation of Israel and a section of that nation. Here also the language is quite conclusive. We are precluded from thinking of the whole nation, for in xlix. 6 the Servant tells us that it is part of his mission ' to raise up the tribes of Jacob, and to restore the preserved of Israel,' and in chapter liii. a plurality of speakers who, as we have seen, are not the Gentiles, and may reasonably be identified with the Jewish nation, speak of the Servant as in some sense distinct from themselves. There can, therefore, be little doubt that by the Lord's Servant we are to understand a section of the Jewish nation.

But this identification of the Servant brings us at once face to face with the problem of the date of these passages. At what period in the history of the Jewish nation did a section of that nation suffer grievous persecution for its steadfastness to the religion of Jehovah, and ultimately win through its struggles a degree of success at which kings were amazed, a success which benefited not only those who had suffered, but also those of their nation who, in the days of the struggle, had sided with the persecutors, and had scorned the martyrs?

It is unnecessary to discuss pre-exilic dates, for both the success which the Servant is said to have achieved, and his attitude towards the Gentiles, are incompatible with what we know of the pre-exilic period; moreover it is almost universally admitted that the prophecies which we have been considering are later than the exile. Our inquiry is therefore narrowed down to the time after the exile, or, to state it more definitely, to the period after the time of Cyrus.

At what time then subsequent to the year 538 B.C. did a section of the Jewish nation suffer persecution for faithfulness to the religion of Jehovah, persecution of which the ultimate cause would seem to be the apostasy of a considerable part of the Jewish nation,

THE SERVANT OF THE LORD 101

and in which Jews were allied with the persecutors ? Such opposition as Zerubbabel and his party encountered from Samaritans and others could hardly be described as religious persecution ; for, if we accept the statement of the book of Ezra, the Samaritans had wished to take part in the building of the Temple ; and, at any rate, the fiercest opposition was directed, not against the Temple, but against the building of the wall of Jerusalem which the prophet Zechariah himself had deprecated. Moreover, at no time during the generation following Zerubbabel's building of the Temple could it have been said of the Jewish community at Jerusalem that their success had astonished kings, and that there was every prospect of their attracting the Gentile world to the religion of Jehovah, so that kings and princes, seeing it, would arise and worship. The age of Zerubbabel will certainly not satisfy the requirements of the exegesis of the prophecies we have considered.

We come then to the age of Nehemiah. Nehemiah was unpopular enough with many of his fellow-countrymen, but he and those who sided with him were never in the condition of absolute helplessness in the presence

102 THE SERVANT OF THE LORD

of their enemies which is implied by the language used of the Servant of the Lord. Certainly the temper of Nehemiah seems very different from that which is ascribed to the Servant. So far from attempting to make Israel a light to the nations, Nehemiah's whole energy was directed towards *isolating Israel from the Gentiles*; and what we know of Judah at the close of his governorship affords us no warrant for supposing that any one in Judah could have used the language of calm triumph and exuberant hope which is found in the 'Servant' passage.

Is there any epoch later in the Persian period which will justify the statements made about the Servant ? The time of Artaxerxes Ochus is considered by many to suit the language of such Psalms as xliv., lxxiv., which speak of the Jews as in dire straits; will it suit the language of the prophecies of the Servant ?

To such a question it is sufficient to say that, even if all that has ever been imagined of the condition of the Jews in the reign of Artaxerxes Ochus were proved to be fact, we should still be unable at this period to account for the language in which the Servant's achieve-

THE SERVANT OF THE LORD 103

ments are described. What great *success* was won for the Jews in the days of Artaxerxes Ochus ? What portion of the nation could say in his reign of any other portion, 'By his stripes *we are healed*' ? Of what section of the Jews could the expectation then be maintained that it would *divide the spoil with the strong* ? Certainly, if we are to look for the interpretation of the prophecies to the circumstances of the Persian period, we can not only say (what, indeed, everybody admits) that the history of this period is very incomplete ; we are justified in affirming that such history of it as we do possess must give an altogether wrong impression.

From the conquest of Palestine by Alexander the Great till the reign of Seleucus IV., 187-176 B.C., there is nothing in the known history of the Jews which will account for the composition of the prophecies on the Servant of the Lord. Before the end of this reign, however, the peace of the Jewish Church was threatened, and in the next reign, that of Antiochus Epiphanes, the Jewish Church was thrown into a furnace of affliction the like of which it had never experienced before.

The facts are briefly these. While

Seleucus IV. was still king, the High Priest, Oniah, who appears to have had the confidence of the anti-Hellenising party, the Hasîdîm as they called themselves, was compelled, owing to certain intrigues against him, to leave Jerusalem for Antioch, in order to set his case before the king. Oniah did not return to Jerusalem, and on the accession of Antiochus Epiphanes his brother Jesus, who had taken the name Jason, was appointed in his stead, he having promised to pay to the Syrian king a larger tribute. Jason was an ardent Helleniser, and he at once set about transforming Jerusalem, which at this time received the name of Antioch, into a Greek city. There is no evidence that Jason and his party were guilty of anything which, in these days, would in itself be considered a serious breach of the Jewish law; but it was impossible for Judaism and Hellenism to be combined without the one or the other being changed; the condition of things in Jerusalem in the days of Jason, though it may not have directly encouraged, provided great temptation to what the Hasîdîm could only look upon as, actual apostasy.

But Jason was not left long in the High

Priesthood which he had usurped. In a short time a Benjamite named Menelaus, backed up by some of the most influential people in Jerusalem and Judaea, intrigued against Jason, and by a money payment induced Antiochus to appoint him High Priest. Menelaus, not being even of priestly family, was quite ineligible for the High Priesthood, and certainly every Jew who retained a spark of reverence for the Law, even though he did not belong to the ranks of the Hasîdîm, must have been scandalised by his appointment. Perhaps Menelaus feared that the general indignation against himself would end in the recall of Oniah at Antioch. To guard against such a contingency he contrived to get Oniah murdered at Antioch.

It was utterly impossible that the Jews should long acquiesce in the High Priesthood of Menelaus. We may feel pretty sure that even the Hasîdîm would be willing to support Jason against him ; for Jason, Helleniser as he was, was, at least by birth, qualified for the High Priesthood. Probably Menelaus had few supporters except among the wealthy Jewish families. The country people belonged, for the most part, to the Hasîdîm.

The turn of events having thus put Jason right with his fellow-countrymen, it was but likely that he should seek to regain his position in Jerusalem. During the campaign of Antiochus in Egypt in 169 B.C., a rumour reached Palestine that the king was dead. Thereupon Jason, who had contrived to collect a thousand men, suddenly marched to Jerusalem, attacked Menelaus, who was compelled to take refuge in the citadel, and massacred a number of his supporters. As Menelaus had been appointed by Antiochus, the latter regarded this attack upon him as a rebellion against his own rule. On his return from Egypt, he brought an army to Jerusalem to vindicate his authority, and to teach the rebellious city a lesson. Jason had already fled, but those who remained bore the full brunt of Antiochus's wrath. There was a massacre of the citizens of Jerusalem by the king's troops, and Antiochus plundered the Temple.

The rising against Menelaus and his supporters, *i.e.* the wealthy Jews who were favourable to the Seleucid government, had made Antiochus doubt the loyalty of the Jewish nation. He determined, therefore, to crush all opposition; and inasmuch as he

THE SERVANT OF THE LORD 107

doubtless knew that the most determined opponents of Menelaus were those who on religious grounds resisted Hellenism, he determined to put a stop to the worship of Jehovah, and to compel the Jews to conform to the worship which he prescribed. In the year 168-167 the Temple, which had suffered already considerably in the struggle between Jason and Menelaus, when the gatehouses had been burnt, was still further desecrated. An image of Olympian Zeus was set up in it, and upon the altar of burnt-offering a Greek altar was placed, on which swine were sacrificed, the High Priest Menelaus taking part in the new ritual. An edict was issued commanding the Jews to take part in the unclean sacrifices, and forbidding to them circumcise their children and to keep the Sabbath. It is evident that many Jews in Jerusalem, no doubt, with inward grief and humiliation, did conform to the king's decree, fearing the penalty of disobedience; but there were not a few even in Jerusalem, and a much larger proportion in the country districts, who were resolved that, come what might, they would not defile themselves with the meat of the sacrifices which the king had commanded, nor bow down to the image which he had set up. It had been the teaching of the fathers, and it was the established doctrine of the Jewish Church, that the Lord would not forsake the righteous, and that the wicked would fall into the pit which he had dug for others. In the circumstances, however, in which the Hasîdîm now found themselves, the old orthodox teaching of retribution broke down. It was on those who were most zealous for the Law of their God that the wrath of Antiochus came to the uttermost. They were perplexed, driven almost into unbelief, and yet they remained faithful. They did not possess the sure and certain hope of a joyful resurrection,[1] and yet they yielded up their bodies to torture and death. The words of Shadrach, Meshach, and Abednego are an example of the faith which in the days of Antiochus inspired thousands of persecuted Jews : ' If our God whom we serve is able to deliver us, from the burning fiery furnace and from thy hand, O king, He will deliver us. But if not, be it known unto thee, O King,

---

[1] 2 Macc. xii. 43 ff. expresses the belief of a later age; and Daniel xii. 2 scarcely warrants the supposition that there was a *common* belief in a general resurrection.

THE SERVANT OF THE LORD

that we will not serve thy gods, nor worship the image which thou hast set up.'

For some time, indeed, it seemed as though the Lord had forsaken His people. The tale of martyrdoms continually grew, and yet the Lord did not interpose. Well might men ask whether there could be any good in prolonging such a struggle; well might they say that they had laboured in vain, and spent their strength for nought and vanity; but though the darkest gloom there broke out the irresistible Hebrew faith, 'Surely my judgment is with the Lord, and my recompence with my God.' Who could deny to such a people the right to style themselves the true Israel, the chosen Servant of the Lord?

And the Lord looked, and there was none to help, and He wondered that there was none to uphold; therefore His own arm brought salvation unto Him, and His fury it upheld Him. Suddenly a great change came over the persecuted people. Those who had suffered mutely turned to resist their enemies. Though they had been counted as sheep for the slaughter, suddenly, under the leadership of the Maccabaean brethren, they became as

110 THE SERVANT OF THE LORD

Jehovah's goodly horse in the battle.[1] I need not dwell on the details of the struggle. Resistance to the troops of Antiochus seemed at first a forlorn hope; but a combination of political circumstances favoured the Maccabees, and enabled them to achieve a success which, at the beginning, had not been dreamed of. Just three years after the desecration of the Temple, it was restored to the Maccabees, who purified it, and rededicated it to the service of Jehovah on the 25th of December 165 B.C. Henceforth the Jews were free to worship as they would. The Maccabaean leaders, however, were not contented with this, and continued the struggle. By throwing in their lot, now with one, now with another of the rival claimants to the throne of Syria, they obtained concession after concession, till in the year 142 B.C., the King of Syria renounced all claim to tribute, and the yoke of the heathen was taken away from Israel. On the 23rd of May 141, the Syrian garrison having at last surrendered, the Maccabees entered the citadel 'with praise and palm branches, and with harps, and with cymbals, and with songs; because a great

[1] Cf. Zech. x. 3.

THE SERVANT OF THE LORD 111

enemy was destroyed out of Israel' (1 Macc. xiii. 51).

It was an occasion which might well have inspired the most phlegmatic; indeed, it probably did inspire words which for their beauty will live for ever.

'Awake, awake, put on thy strength, O Zion; put on thy beautiful garments, O Jerusalem, the holy city : for henceforth there shall no more come into thee the uncircumcised and the unclean. Shake thyself from the dust; arise, sit thee down, O Jerusalem : loose thyself from the bands of thy neck, O captive daughter of Zion.

'For thus saith the LORD, Ye were sold for nought; and ye shall be redeemed without money. For thus saith the Lord GOD, My people went down at the first into Egypt to sojourn there : and the Assyrian[1] oppressed them without cause. Now, therefore, what do I here, saith the LORD, seeing that My people is taken away for nought ? they that rule over them do howl, saith the LORD, and My name continually all the day is blasphemed. Therefore My people shall know My

[1] *i.e.* the Seleucid empire. For this use of אַשּׁוּר cf. Ezra vi. 22; Isa. xi. 16, xix. 23 ff.

name : therefore they shall know in that day that I am He that doth speak ; behold, it is I.

'How beautiful upon the mountains are the feet of him that bringeth good tidings, that publisheth peace, that bringeth good tidings of good, that publisheth salvation ; that saith unto Zion, Thy God reigneth ! The voice of thy watchman ; they lift up the voice, together do they sing ; for they shall see, eye to eye, when the LORD returneth to Zion. Break forth into joy, sing together, ye waste places of Jerusalem : for the LORD hath comforted His people, He hath redeemed Jerusalem. The LORD hath made bare His holy arm in the eyes of all the nations ; and all the ends of the earth shall see the salvation of our God ' (Isaiah lii. 1-10).

The martyred Hasîdîm had not suffered in vain. Even though we cannot see in the Hasmonaean brothers themselves a trace of that whole-hearted piety and devotion to the Law which we see in those who were martyred early in the struggle, through the help which they had obtained from the Hasîdîm the Maccabees had won the freedom of Israel,

THE SERVANT OF THE LORD 113

and had vindicated the Law of Israel. Under Menelaus the national existence itself had been threatened; in the time of Simon the Jews were masters in their own country, and had on all sides extended the borders of their land. Truly it might be said in the days of Simon that the Lord's Servant had raised up the tribes of Jacob, and had restored the preserved of Israel!

But this was not all. When the Jews formed a part of the kingdom of Syria, and the Seleucid government was at war with Egypt, it must have been difficult, if not impossible, for Egyptian Jews to come up to Jerusalem to the feasts. Similarly during the Maccabaean struggle it must have been impossible for Jews who were settled in other portions of the kingdom to visit the district which was in revolt against the king. But when Judaea had become virtually an independent state, the obstacles which had made it well nigh impossible for Jews from Egypt and Assyria to visit Jerusalem were removed. The Lord had made a highway out of Egypt to Assyria, and the Assyrian could come into Egypt, and the Egyptian into Assyria, and the Egyptians could worship with the Assyrians.

The Lord had dried up, as it were, the tongue of the Egyptian sea, and with His scorching wind had He shaken His hand over the river Euphrates, and had smitten it into seven streams so that men could pass over dryshod (cf. Isaiah xi. 15, xix. 23).

And with the establishment of free communication between Jerusalem and the Jews of the Dispersion there came in a kindlier feeling towards the nations of the world. In many a place the leaven of Israel was leavening the lump of heathenism. Those who came up to worship at Jerusalem could tell of many a Gentile who was willing to throw in his lot with the people of the Lord. It had at length come to pass that ten men out of all the languages of the nations would take hold of the skirt of him that was a Jew, saying, We will go with you, for we have heard that God is with you (cf. Zech. viii. 23). Jehovah's Servant, having fulfilled the first part of his destiny, and having raised up the tribes of Jacob, had become a light to lighten the Gentiles.

Such, I believe, is the primary, historical meaning of the prophecies which we have been considering. But since they contain,

THE SERVANT OF THE LORD 115

as I also believe, a divinely inspired interpretation of history, we cannot limit their application to the martyrdom of the Hasîdîm under Antiochus Epiphanes, and the subsequent triumph of the cause for which they suffered, but we must recognise that their teaching possesses a far wider scope. We learn from them that the sufferings of those who, in a wicked or apostate age, endure persecution for their adherence to the right are not in vain. So long as men are ready to endure martyrdom, wickedness cannot have its perfect work. The sight of suffering bravely borne for the truth's sake will cause many, who would otherwise throw in their lot with the wicked, to pause, and then, it may be, to give themselves to the carrying on of the work so nobly begun. In all such cases, to use the language of the Prophets, those who fight for the truth do ' raise up the tribes of Jacob '—the people of the Lord— ' and restore the preserved of Israel '—the ' seven thousand who have not yet bowed the knee to Baal.'

But further, inasmuch as the health of the body politic depends upon righteousness, even those who have had no share in striving for righteousness—those who stand to the righteous in the position in which the Gentiles stood to Israel—are nevertheless benefited by the martyrs' sufferings. It is not only the people of the Lord—the tribes of Jacob—who are raised up and strengthened; those who are beyond the pale, those who walk in darkness like the Gentiles, see the light of the righteous, and thereby receive salvation.

And if this prophetic interpretation of history be applicable to every case of suffering borne for the truth's sake, much more must it be applicable to Him who not only suffered for the truth, but is Himself the truth of God. Surely to all who, having known within themselves the power of that evil which caused the passion and death of Jesus Christ, have experienced the joy of the victory to which His victory pointed the way, and have received within themselves the spirit of adoption whereby they cry, Abba, Father, the words of the Hebrew Prophet receive a deeper meaning; they are indeed 'fulfilled' in Christ. It would scarcely be possible to sum up the work of Christ more tersely than in the words of the great prophecy which we have been considering: 'He was wounded

THE SERVANT OF THE LORD 117

for our transgressions, He was bruised for our iniquities : the chastisement of our peace was upon Him ; and with His stripes we are healed.'

But since there may be some who, though they are quite prepared to accept the theory of a primary, historical reference in the prophecies which form the subject of these lectures, may yet feel difficulty in assigning any part of the book of Isaiah to a date as late as I have postulated, it may be well that I should say a few words on this point.[1] The facts are briefly these. That a book of Isaiah was in existence at the beginning of the second century B.C., and that Isaiah was included among the canonical Prophets seems certain from Ecclus. xlviii. 22 ff. ; but it does not follow that this book was identical with that which we now possess. It is certain that the Hebrew book of Jeremiah was re-edited after the Greek translation of it was made ; and if one book of the Prophets could be re-edited after it was translated into Greek, it is not easy to see what insuperable objection there

---

[1] For a fuller treatment of this question I may refer to my Schweich Lectures—*The Composition of the Book of Isaiah in the Light of History and Archæology.*

can be to a theory which requires us to believe that another book was translated into Greek shortly after the issue of a new edition of the Hebrew. Exactly what was contained in the book of Isaiah known to Ben Sira cannot be decided with certainty. He mentions the going backward of the sun in the days of Isaiah; but we are unable to say whether he derived this fact from the book of Isaiah or from the book of Kings. The only passage of the prophetical portion of the book which Ben Sira seems to refer to at all definitely is the section lxi. 1 ff.

Some seventy or eighty years later, as we learn from the prologue to Ecclesiasticus written by the grandson of the author, all three divisions of the Hebrew Canon, the Law, the Prophets, and the Hagiographa, were represented in a Greek version of the Scriptures; and although we cannot suppose that the whole of the Old Testament had been translated into Greek at this time, it is likely that, if any of the prophets had been translated, Isaiah would be among the number. But it must be noted that the author of the preface does not say that he found the Prophets translated *when he arrived in Egypt*

THE SERVANT OF THE LORD 119

in the thirty-eighth year of Euergetes. All that can be established from his words is that a translation of this part of the Old Testament existed *when he published his own version* of his grandfather's book. And the fact that the Jewish Church in Egypt accepted the Greek version of Ecclesiasticus among its Scriptures, though the Church at Jerusalem never regarded the original book as canonical, may be taken as evidence that the Greek translation of the greater portion of the Old Testament had not been in the possession of the Jews in Egypt for any length of time. Had this been the case, had the canonical books been marked as distinct from other literature, the inclusion of the book in the Egyptian canon would be hard to explain. We do not know the exact meaning of the word συγχρονίσας (translated in R. V. 'having continued there some time'); but if, as Mr. Hart suggests,[1] it means 'having stayed there as long as Euergetes reigned,' the date of the publication of Ecclesiasticus will be not earlier than 117 B.C. Since there is no prophecy in the book of Isaiah which it is necessary to assign to a later date than 141

[1] Hart, *Ecclesiasticus in Greek*, p. 259.

B.C., there would thus be an interval of more than twenty years between the composition of its latest portions and the translation of the whole book into Greek. This would allow ample time for the editing of the book in Jerusalem or Judaea, and for the book so edited to be taken to Egypt and there translated. But even if the sense assigned to συγχρονίσας be inadmissible; even if the translator of Ecclesiasticus published his work within two years of his arrival in Egypt; we have an interval of some ten years between the date of the latest prophesy and the time when there is evidence of the existence of the Greek version of the book of Isaiah, and much may be done in ten years.

In order to give some idea of the time necessary for the translation of the Prophets and Hagiographa, we may take an illustration from our own time. The Revision of the whole of the Old Testament in English, which was begun on June 30, 1870, was completed on June 20, 1884. But in this case, of necessity the work was not continuous. The number of days actually devoted to the work was seven hundred and ninety-two. If then a large body of scholars, who were compelled to discuss at length differences of opinion as to the rendering of the work to be translated, could complete the whole of the Old Testament in seven hundred and ninety-two days, there is no difficulty in supposing that a version of the Old Testament, exclusive of the Pentateuch and of some books of the Hagiographa, could be completed by a body of translators working independently [1] in even less time, and there would still remain ample time for the editing of the original Hebrew text.

Finally, it cannot be insisted upon too strongly that, when we have once abandoned the traditional view of the authorship of Isaiah, the son of Amoz, there is no reason for preferring a date during the Exile to the Maccabaean period, if the latter is in harmony with all the facts. Why should it be imagined that God could inspire men during the fifth century B.C. and during the first century of the Christian era, but not in the intervening period? Is it not far more reasonable, far more faithful to believe that the promise of Deut. xviii. 15 was fulfilled all through the

[1] *N.B.*—That the various books of the Old Testament were translated by different hands is certain (Swete, *Introduction to the Old Testament in Greek*, p. 315 ff.

Old Dispensation, as indeed it has been, and still is, fulfilled in the New? Throughout the ages 'the true light, even the light which lighteth every man,' has been 'coming into the world.'

www.ingramcontent.com/pod-product-compliance
Lightning Source LLC
Chambersburg PA
CBHW070501100426
42743CB00010B/1716